The Pandemic Information Gap

The Pandemic Information Gap

The Brutal Economics of COVID-19

Joshua Gans

The MIT Press

Cambridge, Massachusetts | London, England

Some material included in *The Pandemic Information Gap* was previously published in the MIT Press eBook *Economics in the Age of COVID-19*.

This book was set in Stone Serif and Stone Sans by Jen Jackowitz. Printed and bound in the United States of America.

Library of Congress Cataloging-in-Publication Data

Names: Gans, Joshua, 1968- author.
Title: The pandemic information gap : the brutal economics of COVID-19 / Joshua Gans.
Description: Cambridge, Massachusetts : The MIT Press, [2020] | Includes bibliographical references.
Identifiers: LCCN 2020028165 | ISBN 9780262539128 (paperback)
Subjects: MESH: Coronavirus Infections--economics | Pneumonia, Viral--economics | Communication | Pandemics--economics
Classification: LCC RA644.C67 | NLM WC 505 | DDC 362.1962/41400681--dc23
LC record available at https://lccn.loc.gov/2020028165

10   9   8   7   6   5   4   3   2   1

To my economist colleagues who dropped everything to work on COVID-19 issues. They showed the way for our governments to act with unprecedented urgency and fortitude. There are many in society who deserve and have received acclaim, but your work has been more hidden than most. Our good economic management of the crisis (and this book) would not have been possible without you.

Contents

Preface

On September 26, 2001, *The Onion* headline read, "Not Knowing What Else to Do, Woman Bakes American-Flag Cake."[1] That was the feeling I had at the onset of the COVID-19 pandemic in March 2020. I found myself unable to get work done and constantly obsessing over news and then data on topics that I knew very little about. I was in self-isolation, having traveled to the United States. Upon reflection, not knowing what else to do, I decided I would do what I was good at: I'd write a book. I would endeavor to explain some of the broader economic issues arising from the pandemic to a wide audience.

In this task, I was hampered by two things. First, and this is what every economist writing about this has been saying, I am not an epidemiologist. That meant I was absorbing that material as an amateur and so had to be cautious regarding my own understanding. So, I would be flying well beyond what the usual academic norms would dictate, which meant I had to be careful in making any claims. That said, my goal here was to explain the economic issues of all this, and in that task, I am very experienced. Second, things were moving fast. Policies were changing. Scientists were learning more about the virus and its disease. No one had the information to create an appropriate assessment to evaluate the reasonableness of decisions being made, although everyone (including myself) had opinions they were willing to put all over social media. But if this book was going to be relevant in a month, let alone a year's time, I was going to have to refrain from being judgmental. That meant that there would be no politics, political economy, or even applause for what seemed like the best policies nor disdain for what seemed like the worst. Readers looking for that will have to go elsewhere.

This is a significantly revised version of the book that I wrote at the beginning of the crisis in March 2020 entitled *Economics in the Age of COVID-19*. Despite being almost double in length, it remains a book written in that same crisis just two months on. Its purpose is to be an urgent source of clarification and a thoughtful take on the issues. I had to forecast what we would potentially take away from this crisis and what we would want to reflect on beyond the chaos of the first few months. I'm hoping not to be completely wrong about all of that, but if I am, I will be the first one to call it out.

I would like to thank my family with whom I am stuck in a house writing this. They put up with my crazy idea to push out a book when I could be less socially distant, at least inside our household. I would also like to thank Scott Adams, Ajay Agrawal, Pierre Azoulay, Heski Bar-Isaac, Franceso Bova, Kevin Bryan, Eric Budish, Bruce Chapman, Ben Fine, Catherine de Fontenay, Laura Derkson, Alberto Galasso, Avi Goldfarb, Steve Hamilton, Richard Holden, Bill Janeway, Chris Joye, Stephen King, Scott Kominers, Mara Lederman, Andrew Leigh, June Ma, Tiff Macklem, Barry Nalebuff, Bob Pindyck, Eric Rasmusen, Paul Romer, Andrew Steck, Scott Stern, Alex Tabarrok, and Flavio Toxvaerd for helpful comments and discussions. A special thanks for commenters on PubPub (in particular, Patty Steele) with their many suggestions that improved the book. I would also like to thank my constant companion through this—#econtwitter—who alerted me to much of the research cited in this book. Finally, I owe a special debt to Emily Taber and the MIT Press team for acting so quickly to get this project out there.

—July 2020

1
All about Information

Everything is awful. The virus is awful. The immediate choices are awful. The future may be even more awful.

We should have been more prepared. For almost a decade, one of the most popular apps was *Plague Inc.* (120 million downloads and counting). It showed us how diseases broke out and did their damage. When the COVID-19 outbreak hit, the app surged back to number one in China and was promptly banned in the country.[1]

In *Plague Inc.*, you play the virus and your goal is to wipe out humanity. To the extent they have a goal, that isn't the goal of most viruses. Instead, it might be survival of its genetic structure, which would end should it wipe out its hosts. But never mind; from humanity's perspective, we would want to tool up on the tactics for viruses that would lead to extinction.[2]

COVID-19 is not that species-ending virus. But it does have some of the characteristics you would employ in *Plague Inc.* if you wanted to destroy us all. An inexperienced player normally goes for a highly infectious and deadly disease. But that is not the best course of action. First, because the virus is deadly, human scientists start working extra hard to stop the plague. Second, if you kill people too quickly, you actually slow down the rate of infection. Instead, what you want to do is find a way of infecting many people preferably without any symptoms that would get the infection noticed. Then you want to ramp up the disease after each infected person has spread it around so that you overwhelm health centers before the world shuts down travel.

If the key to winning *Plague Inc.* is to move in stealth so as not to provoke an effective human response, then COVID-19 fits that bill. People become infectious, many with zero or just mild symptoms, but then there is a deadly movement into pneumonia and other serious problems, which takes some weeks of hospitalization to treat. There is an information problem that prevents a targeted response. If we had known who was infected, we could have kept them from others and monitored their health for signs of problems. But COVID-19, being carried by people free of symptoms, kept that information hidden.

By obscuring its prevalence, COVID-19 gets high marks for being able to spread quickly through the population. While this is not necessarily enough to win *Plague Inc.*, COVID-19 was able to crash the world economy to levels not seen since the Great Depression and make people afraid to come out again. In that respect, it was the pandemic that games, TED talks, books, and medical reports were trying to warn us about for years.[3] And it was a real game that likely would last for some time.

A Lack of Knowledge Is Infectious

COVID-19 is a disease caused by a novel coronavirus, SAR-CoV-2, that itself can pass from person to person. Suppose, for the moment, that you had perfect knowledge of whether any particular individual was infected or not. To give you a picture, imagine the virus was such that it inflated people's noses and made them shine bright red like Rudolph the Red-Nosed Reindeer. Imagine also that, as those people moved, they left a trail of red you could see even after a number of hours. Then anyone could easily identify who is safe to interact with and who is not. For those who are unsafe, we could isolate them or approach them only if they or you had suitable protective gear. We are not passive organisms in spreading a virus. With knowledge, we can take action. It is a lack of knowledge that makes the coronavirus infectious and a threat to the world.

The contention in this book is that, at their heart, pandemics are an information problem. Solve the information problem and you can defeat the virus. There is a big difference between knowing someone you interact with is infectious and having to make a guess as to whether that person is infectious. In the former case, you can act and limit the interactions. In the latter case, you have to take a risk. And, in evaluating that risk, what we care about is not just whether you become infected but also whether you might pass that infection on to others.

The difference between perfect knowledge and no knowledge is what causes an infectious disease to have an impact on social and economic interactions. With perfect knowledge, some people get sick, they are isolated, and life is (for most of us) essentially unchanged. With no knowledge at all and no interventions to prevent infections, then for COVID-19, at its peak, about 21 million people in the United States alone would likely be infectious at one time. With no restrictions on activity, the probability that you interact with one of the infectious people on a given day is 21 million divided by 327 million (the US population), or 6.4 percent.[4] However, suppose you interact with only 10 people per week. In that situation, the probability that you are able to avoid any of those infected people is about 50-50. When going to public spaces, you may interact with over a hundred people per week. In that case, your probability of avoiding an infected person becomes close to zero. In other words, perfect knowledge allows you to avoid *all* infected people. No knowledge makes it near certain that you will encounter at least one infected person.

Without knowledge of how many people are infected and whether particular people are carriers of the coronavirus, we are forced to take drastic actions. We have to blindly swing a hammer at the virus in the hope of preventing infections from spreading. When the virus is spreading through the population and we don't know where it is concentrated, we are forced into just keeping everyone apart—through social distancing or a lockdown—basically, as if every person was actually infected even when, in actuality, few are. It is as if we know there are a couple of deadly spiders living in our house, but we don't know where and, in order to make the house safe, we are forced to burn it down. In other words, if it looks like our actions to combat the spread of disease are overkill, it is because they are. If we knew more, we could tailor our response and save ourselves the vast majority of grief we have endured in 2020.

Possible Endgames

A pandemic has a number of possible endgames and some are definitely more attractive than others. *Which endgame we achieve depends critically on how quickly and effectively we solve the pandemic information problem.* So, let's look at our endgame options.[5]

The first candidate endgame is to develop and distribute a vaccine for the coronavirus. In effect, the idea is to outsource the job of managing the information problem to antibodies that identify and kill the virus should it enter the body. The right antibody will bind itself to the coronavirus in the body and make it inactive. Hence, it cannot do harm, reproduce, or spread to others. A vaccine seeds the development of those antibodies in a person. The other way a person can get antibodies is by being infected and their own immune system successfully neutralizing the virus. Thus, a vaccine is a preemptive defense against the coronavirus that avoids the body having to fight the coronavirus itself, and all the collateral damage to the body that can entail.[6] For this reason, having a vaccine would be a preferred endgame for COVID-19.

At the time of writing, health researchers are confident but not certain that the body can generate antibodies that can continue to neutralize the virus. For the same reason, they do not know if they can create a safe vaccine to do the job. The assumption is that this is possible, and it is only a matter of time. But it is also possible that might never happen. In that case, the pandemic could be endemic and be with us for a long time with people becoming sick at regular intervals. Given the optimistic projections, in this book I will presume that a vaccine is on the horizon and that, if you have contracted the coronavirus and survived, then you are immune, not infectious, and no longer a potential future carrier. Where necessary, I will comment on what might happen if that presumption turns out to be false.

If the coronavirus does make those who were infected subsequently immune, there is a second endgame scenario for COVID-19: enough people become immune that the virus is no longer able to spread in an uncontrolled manner throughout the population. To be sure, the early arrival of a vaccine could preempt this endgame, but let's consider what is involved in it playing out.

During the early stages of a pandemic, there are few people infected in the population, but for an infectious virus like the coronavirus, the number of people starts to grow exponentially. That means that the number of infections increases in a compounding way—each new infected person infects some others who then infect more and so on. But that can go on for only so long. Infected people eventually, if they should survive, become immune and no longer can spread the virus. With fewer people to go to, the growth phase goes into reverse. Epidemiologists call that reversal point the time at which the population achieves "herd immunity." For the coronavirus, that point is when about 60 percent of a population are immune.[7] Infections still continue to rise after that point because the virus is still circulating—it just no longer is growing exponentially. Eventually, when about 87 percent of the population are immune, the virus will die out.[8] (This is also the same proportion of the population that need to be vaccinated at the onset to prevent the virus from taking off in the first place.)

This is the endgame where we do nothing and pretend the virus does not exist—including modifying our own behavior to reduce the risk of infection. This would seem to be simple—let our own immune system do all of the work. The problem is that this process will take about a year and for COVID-19 could lead to 1 percent or more of those infected not surviving. For a city with a population of 1 million, that would add up to almost 9,000 dead and, at its peak, 90,000 people in hospital which would require beds and other facilities at the rate of 90 for every 1,000 people or so. For comparison, South Korea, a country at the top of the ranks in hospital capacity, has 13.4 beds per 1,000, while the United States has 2.9. In other words, there are likely to be many more deaths in reality in this endgame as healthcare systems are overrun.

In reality, the endgame that lets the virus "run its course" would not actually play out in this way. First of all, people would change their own behavior and that would reduce the rate of infections. Second, as we saw around the world, governments would mandate social distancing policies, which reinforced the direction people themselves were heading. These actions would "flatten the curve"; basically, pushing out the time the peak of infections occurred so that hospitals were not overrun. If this was done perfectly, then in the end there would be less than 87 percent of the population infected and there would be fewer fatalities as hospitals could cope better, but this may take up to three years before the virus dies out. All that time, the economic and social price of the crisis would have to be paid. The only thing that might cut the process short is the arrival of the vaccine and switching to that endgame.

There is a final endgame that can avoid all of this grief and obviate the need for a vaccine or the "run its course" outcomes: suppression. Even a very infectious virus can be made to die out well before a significant share of the population become infected. In 2002, the first coronavirus epidemic caused by the virus SARS-CoV-1, or as it was then known, just SARS, emerged. SARS is far more dangerous than COVID-19 and, on average, would kill 10 percent of the people it infected. It was also more infectious than its successor, spreading very quickly through hospitals and other areas infected people had passed through. But in the end only about 8,500 people worldwide were known to have contracted SARS with those cases concentrated in China, Hong Kong, Taiwan, Singapore, and Canada. Some 774 people were known to have died. In other words, SARS was contained and suppressed well before it had run its course or any vaccine was developed.

How was this endgame achieved? SARS itself helped us along. While SARS incubated in people for a few days, it became infectious only when they developed a fever and other flu-like symptoms. These could be easily observed; not quite an inflated red nose but close. People suspected of being infected with SARS could be quickly isolated. Because of this, it took only a month or so for the virus to be contained and another few months for it to be suppressed completely. No new cases have been reported since 2004. In other words, SARS allowed the pandemic information problem to be resolved very quickly. By doing so, the epidemic was suppressed before it caused worldwide harm, although it did disrupt travel to and from Asia for a number of months. If infections from COVID-19 can fall to low enough levels, suppression will be achieved.[9]

The message here is simple: **solve the pandemic information problem, save the world**. COVID-19 appeared in November 2019. As of March 2020, the opportunity to contain COVID-19 to a few countries was well and truly lost. For a country to adopt the suppression endgame would have required preemptive management of the pandemic information problem. So long as the number of infections in a population is relatively low, this can be achieved by identifying infected people quickly (through testing and contact tracing) and then quarantining them or isolating them. The problem is that when too many of the population are already infected, the costs of identifying people in this way become too high—they do not, as we say, scale. In this situation, more hammer-like strategies like large-scale social distancing need to be taken to manage the virus or bring the number of infections down to a level that would allow the suppression endgame to be pursued.[10]

Phases of the Pandemic Economy

The following chapters are structured along the lines of various phases that arise for the economy during a pandemic. The four phases are illustrated in figure 1.1. The overarching goal is to reduce the rate of infection such that the pandemic ends. But how this is done has differential impacts on health versus wealth. How those should be prioritized is the subject of chapter 2. There it is argued that epidemiological insights favor prioritizing health over wealth as we try to learn more about the properties and impact of COVID-19.

The remainder of the book is devoted to how to actively manage the pandemic information problem. The idea is to get to a position where the pandemic information problem can be managed for

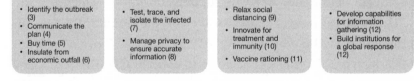

Figure 1.1
The phases of the pandemic economy

suppression or to buy enough time for a vaccine to be developed. Nonetheless, how precisely that endgame is achieved—that is, how a sufficient share of the population becomes immune—involves choices that will be outlined in the chapters that follow.

The first phase of the pandemic economy shown in figure 1.1 is **containment**. This involves four steps. The first, as already noted, is that the virus, outbreak, and potential pandemic have to be identified. This is the subject of chapter 3. While this is going on, the pandemic is playing itself out unabated. Chapter 4 then argues why communication is critical during this stage. You want to ensure that the public is receiving information from trusted sources so the public can act on that information without the authorities having to resort to blanket and costly enforcement of people's activities.

Following this is a step that is designed to put the brakes on and stop the virus from spreading. This is the initial part of holding the line to learn more about the virus and to preserve potentially scarce economic resources. The decisions that must be made then are akin to those made by governments during wartime. They involve immediate sacrifice, and, as I point out in chapter 5, they require an approach to resource allocation that would, at all other times, be considered repugnant: centrally planned economies. But this is where governments, appropriately, have started to act. There are centralized and military-run operations to improve healthcare system capacity. There are price controls and subsequent rationing. And there are blanket restrictions on movement. None of these things would have been achievable under a free market regime, and all of these actions have the potential to save many lives and ultimately preserve our economy.

The costs of those decisions are very hard to fathom. Perhaps the largest contraction in economic activity since the Great Depression is taking place. And this is by choice so we could reduce the spread of COVID-19. The impact of that has been unevenly felt with growing numbers of unemployed and bankruptcies from small- and medium-sized businesses occurring. How to use government policy—both fiscal and monetary—is not simple.[11] In chapter 6, I explain that this type of recession is very different from past recessions and requires a distinct approach. The goal would be to somehow *pause* the economy so that it could be later unpaused and life could return to normal. Thus, we wouldn't let businesses fail and people lose their jobs. They need to be insulated. We need policies—in particular, loans—to keep people from breaking economic relationships either because businesses shut down or jobs are shed.

If COVID-19 is successfully contained, the next phase is to **reset** everything and start from scratch.[12] This is where we start to tackle the pandemic information problem head on by acquiring information that helps us predict which individuals are likely to be infected and to isolate them from others. In chapter 7, I describe this reset phase as a move to a testing economy. In that economy, we test widely to determine who is safe to interact with others. Then we *repeat* that until such time as a vaccine is distributed or the virus has otherwise abated. In this way, moving to a testing economy can expand our production possibilities. This is what we would have liked to do at the outset but lacked either the information or the means to do so. It highlights that the role of the containment phase is effectively to get us back to square one and have a "do over" based on better knowledge going forward. This will, however, involve dealing with issues of privacy that become particularly salient when it comes to the disclosure to public health authorities of the health status of individuals. How privacy concerns can be managed is the topic of chapter 8.

Having reset and developed a means of testing, we will be able to begin the **recovery** phase from the pandemic. In chapter 9, I consider the economic issues associated with reemergence. There will be a need to prioritize who is released from isolation, as not all of the population will be designated safe for interactions. This is based on network theory, which can give us guidance as to what types of jobs, workplaces, and other factors can serve as criteria for release. In reemergence we will also face rationing of certain things—most notably, vaccine doses—and will need to consider how those scarce resources are allocated.

Chapter 10 then looks at a related but also ongoing part of the recovery: the need to rally innovation. Innovations will be needed for tests, treatments, and vaccines for COVID-19 but also for dealing with pandemics in the future. The fundamental problem is that these innovations are global public goods that we want wide distribution of, but the urgency and other factors mean that normal market-based processes of innovating are not going to succeed. Instead, I discuss various tools that might accelerate innovations, including advance market commitments to purchase the products based on innovations. These can overcome some of the incentive-dampening pressures that might otherwise emerge for innovators in this area.

If we have a vaccine for the coronavirus, then what? While there are options available to accelerate production and distribution of vaccine doses, the sheer scale of the endeavor means that it is highly likely there will be shortages. Markets can be used to deal with this situation with higher prices being charged for those who obtain doses earlier, as with much of healthcare. Chapter 11 argues that this will likely be an unacceptable process. Instead, governments will opt for a big rationing. The chapter explores how this might be achieved. Will governments make a list of people who will have priority? Will they hold a lottery to distribute doses to the remainder of the population? Is it a good idea to allow lottery tickets to be resold? These are all tough issues with trade-offs between efficiency and equity that governments will have to grapple with.

Finally, having evolved from the current crisis we will reach a new phase: the future (chapter 12). My assumption here is that, like major crises of the past, we will want to find ways to avoid them in the future. We will need to **prepare** for the next pandemic. There are opportunities for global cooperation and also to consider the differential impact of these crises and their resolution on different groups. Thus, I will end the book reflecting on these but noting that much of the work outlining that truly does lie in our future.

Key Points

1. Pandemics are information problems. If we knew who was infected, we could isolate them and prevent viruses from becoming pandemics.

2. The endgame for pandemics is either the discovery of an effective vaccine, having it run its course, or suppressing it.

3. Suppression is preferable to mitigate both the health and economic costs of a pandemic but achieving it relies on confronting and managing the pandemic information problem early.

4. In dealing with the pandemic, governments must first contain the outbreak in order to then put themselves in a position to reset and conduct recovery policies—such as testing and tracing and innovations in treatment and prevention—in order to bring the crisis to a resolution.

2

Health before Wealth

We know what to do to bring our economy back to life. What
we do not know how to do is to bring people back to life.
—His Excellency William Addo Dankwa "Nana" Akufo-Addo,
President of Ghana, March 26, 2020[1]

There is no more brutal trade-off than trying to make life and death
decisions with dollar costs attached. And, as is often the case, there
are no people more annoying in confronting that trade-off than
economists. Only an economist could watch the movie *The Martian*
and wonder whether spending what must have been several billion
dollars was worth it just for the chance of rescuing Matt Damon.

In normal times, economists do these calculations unapolo-
getically. They relentlessly focus on the fact that we have limited
resources and can do only so much. If we direct expenditures
toward, say, public health, we are giving up something else. Thus,
it was not surprising to see some economists reminding people of
those trade-offs with respect to the COVID-19 pandemic.

"We put a lot of weight on saving lives," said Casey Mulligan,
a University of Chicago economist who spent a year as chief

economist on Mr. Trump's Council of Economic Advisers. "But it's not the only consideration. That's why we don't shut down the economy every flu season. They're ignoring the costs of what they're doing. They also have very little clue how many lives they're saving."[2]

This has the effect of causing some politicians and business leaders to embrace the notion that in dealing with a pandemic, we need to be conscious that if we push for public health, we are trading that off against a loss in economic health.

The technique of "thinking at the margin" often serves us well. This is because we can narrow the argument and think in terms of tweaking or fine tuning where we are now. In dealing with trade-offs, the economist asks, If we get a little more of something, how much of something else do we have to give up? In this case, thinking at the margin would ask, If we want to open up the economy a little more during a pandemic, how many lives would that cost? Trade-offs (especially at the margin) are the economist's bread and butter. So, it really shouldn't surprise us to see this being voiced during a time of pandemic.

However, this misses a critical issue: pandemics are not the time where trade-offs at the margin are appropriate. That does not remove the question of how to balance the needs of the economy with the needs of public health. But it does cause our normal economic intuition to be refined. The good news is that this can be done by integrating a simple epidemiological model[3] with basic economic analysis.

What Epidemiology Tells Us

The starting point is to understand that, at any given point in time, there is only so much we can produce. Broadly speaking, if we want to have better public health outcomes, we need to take resources from elsewhere, and so we can imagine that we get less of other stuff—which we would broadly call "the economy." What makes these trade-offs easy to grasp is that when we talk about producing some more public health, we can then think about how much less of the economy we get. Moreover, we are also confident that as we push for each extra bit of health, the more of the economy we have to give up each time. So, if our public health is poor, it is relatively "cheap" (in terms of a reduction in the economy) to get more of it. When our public health is already prioritized, pushing the system further to gain even more health is relatively "expensive" in terms of reductions to the economy. Thus, we do end up balancing and we don't have the best imaginable public health outcomes because, frankly, we have decided not to pay the price. (In the technical interlude at the end of this chapter, I put all of this discussion in graphical terms that might be familiar to an Econ 101 student—the production possibilities frontier. You can delve into that or skip as you see fit.)

One reason a pandemic is brutal is because it constrains even further what we can do with our scarce resources. We can neither sustain the level of the economy we had before without a decline in public health nor vice versa. That in and of itself would not pose an issue for our ability to fine tune. Instead, there are two factors that fundamentally mean that we can no longer fine tune and instead face a choice between prioritizing public health or the economy without the ability to balance those choices. Those two factors are (1) that a pandemic *hollows out* our ability to maintain the *same* balance between health and the economy and (2) that our choice of priority changes our options going forward; that is, they can drift.

Let's begin with hollowing out. Recall that our ability to obtain our current balance of health and the economy is that we recognize that having a little more health or a little more economy is not worth the price in terms of what we give up for each. Absent other innovations—say, a vaccine or, as I will discuss later, testing—the way to achieve our previous level of public health in the face of a pandemic is to socially distance. That means that we cannot physically interact with one another, and, therefore, to a very large extent, we can no longer produce the economic outcomes we once could.

The problem is that the pandemic now changes the price of obtaining a little improvement in the economy. In order to do that, we must now give up a large degree of health as the infection rate of COVID-19 is high. Being able to have slightly larger groups of people interact or have a few workplaces open poses a potentially high risk to public health because of the way the coronavirus can spread. Put simply, the option of sacrificing a little public health for having a little more economy is no longer open to us.

This also works on the flip side. One option for dealing with a pandemic is simply to ignore it and let life go on as usual. The hope from that plan would be to maintain the economy at its previous level, see the virus spread through much of the population, hope not too many people die, and have a one- to two-year large decline in public health. This was sometimes referred to as allowing the virus to "burn through" the population. Even here the ability to fine tune is compromised. You might want to achieve a slightly lower loss of life from the pandemic but find now that the price of doing that, as even that would require a large amount of social distancing, has become very high.

Hollowing out means that you no longer want to maintain the same balance of the economy and health as you did previously. Instead, the "best" choices are to prioritize one or the other. There is a trade-off, but no longer can you dial up a little bit more of this and a little bit less of that; you either prioritize the economy or you prioritize public health. You don't want to try to do both.

One thing that can tip the balance is that you may not be able to maintain the economy at its previous level if you just let the pandemic burn through the population. This is because, like a war or natural disaster, we lose resources if we have much lower public health; that is, our workforce becomes smaller. Thus, if we let a pandemic run its course without mitigation that lowers economic activity, what happens is what I call a "dark recession." This is a recession where we see a reduction in the availability, ability, and health of the workforce as the virus spreads unabated. This causes a large reduction in economic activity.[4]

Put in this way, at the onset of a pandemic, societies face a choice. They can direct their policies to prioritize public health—at least, insofar as it relates to how the virus itself impacts on that health—or they can prioritize the promotion of economic activity. Thus, even though there is a trade-off, it is not at the margin (a little bit of health for a little bit of economic activity); it is more like one or the other (do you want to save lives or save the economy?).[5] We do have some handle on the cost of engaging in extreme social distancing by ending nonessential economic activity. One study estimated that non-extreme social distancing in the United States during 2020 would reduce real GDP by 11 percent (or $2.25 trillion) that year.[6] Another estimated that $375 billion per month in global wealth was being lost.[7] Keeping fatalities to a minimum would likely involve even more of a reduction in GDP. That is a large enough number to give some people pause as to whether it is worth it. Although before exploring whether severe economic constrictions are worth it to save lives, we must first understand the other side of that equation. I should anticipate that there is an issue with this particular framing in terms of a ledger of numbers for and against, and it relates to the information issues that are at the core of this book. I will address that informational issue shortly.

What's a Life Worth?

Suppose, however, that it was a straight-out horse race between $2.25 trillion (in the United States at least) and the number of lives that sacrifice would save. How would we run that horse race?

Historically, economists were somewhat reluctant participants in such calculations. Going back to Wilfred Pareto (the great mathematician and economist of the late nineteenth century), the economic approach to approving of a course of action is to ask whether that action makes some people better off without making *any* others worse off. If the answer was yes, then surely the action was worthwhile. The problem is that the answer was rarely positive. When it came to issues of health, no one could argue that even a single fatality passed the Pareto test. Somewhat uncomfortably, however, society demonstrated all the time that no one life, or even several lives, had veto power over the economy.

While economists were out of the picture, those lobbying against certain safety regulations started to assign numbers to lives. One popular route was to value an individual's life in terms equivalent to their earning potential. This was something often employed by courts in valuing damages in liability matters. The problem was that money was not everything, and not everyone who lived had monetary earnings. Lives were much more. Thus, economists needed to do better if only to be persuasive on why lives should have a higher value than some were assigning them. Macabre though this is, the intent was to force policy makers to at least take into account loss of life in their calculations, which otherwise too easily could be ignored.

Economists Thomas Schelling and Kip Viscusi are the most celebrated of those who suggest that if we look at people's risky behavior (activities that people know might lead to death), we could estimate the value they were placing on their own lives (for instance, by looking at wage differentials for working in certain construction jobs or in security). This is the value of a statistical life. Numerous government agencies have put that value at between $5 million and $10 million as of 2020.[8] If that is the case, then for pandemics of even modest size, the loss-of-life component dwarfs the economic cost.[9] Put simply, in our horse race, it would be worth losing $2.25

trillion in US GDP if it could save more than 225,000 lives. Given that an unchecked COVID-19 pandemic had been predicted to take between one and two million lives, the race was not close. The cure certainly did not look worse than the disease.[10]

One objection to this calculation is that COVID-19 did not cause death equally among different demographic segments of the population. Indeed, fatalities were concentrated among the elderly.[11] Some argued that this should adjust the value of life calculations downward because, put simply, the expected number of years of life for senior citizens was lower than average.[12] To those who believe a life is a life, such adjustments seem abhorrent. However, ask yourself, Had the virus disproportionately taken the lives of children—as they often do—would you have still been happy to use the population average as their value of life? Hard as it is to admit, we do consider the lives yet to live in thinking about such matters. Nonetheless, as it turns out, research revealed that, on average, people dying from COVID-19 were losing a decade of their lives and so were hardly near death.[13] This too masks any permanent health issues (such as reduced lung function) that may arise.

While these calculations suggest we have a considerable buffer in choosing to prioritize health over wealth, at the outset, there was considerable uncertainty. First, it was not at all clear what the fatality rate of COVID-19 was and if it could be mitigated by treatments or the provision of medical equipment such as ventilators. Second, it was equally not clear what some of the public health costs were from dealing the pandemic as medical resources would be shifted away from other things and toward dealing with pandemic care. After all, while some surgeries are elective, it is only a matter of time before they turn into something more urgent. Finally, even reductions in economic activity can have health consequences, including degradations in mental health.[14] In the end, while economists have played a role in assigning a value to life and these have been used in raw cost–benefit analysis, the subjective and moral issues suggest that making those calls is best left to others or, at least, a democratically broad constituency.[15]

The Drift

In addition to uncertainty regarding the fatality rate, healthcare disruptions, and the health consequences of recessions, there were other factors affecting what the choice between prioritizing health over the economy might be. In particular, we did not know how hard the pandemic was to contain. For instance, was a complete lockdown required or some more modest strategies such as prohibitions on public events and discouraging travel or anything between? And if there were costs associated with measures to reduce the infection rate, what things might be done to mitigate those costs? In particular, what economic measures were needed to prevent long-term disruptions to the economy (an issue we return to in chapter 5)? And, indeed, just how difficult will be the short-term economic hardship? There were an incredible number of unknown factors, and while a raw, back-of-the-envelope calculation may have pointed to health prioritization, the details of that were far from clear along many dimensions.

Faced with uncertainty, what you want to do is keep your options open. If it turns out economic costs are much higher than anticipated, you want the option to reprioritize economic factors. Alternatively, if the health consequences of less extreme policies are more dire than anticipated, you want to be able to reprioritize health without too much difficulty. In a normal situation, this might be a choice in the face of uncertainty where you can freely adjust your strategy as you learn more. However, epidemiological models have another implication that suggests the choice is more difficult than a judgment call. The options can *drift* depending on how we respond to the pandemic. Put simply, the longer you take to enact more intense social distancing, the fewer options you have.

This means that you can no longer achieve the existing level of health and must accept less.

This is the drift. Your ability to generate higher levels of public health during the pandemic is reduced unless you commit to holding the line on health. Importantly, if you spend too long trying to maintain the previous balance between the economy and public health, you are unable to achieve better levels of public health at all.

Importantly, the drift goes in only one direction. If you choose to prioritize the economy and maintain previous levels of economic activity, you may cut off the option of improving public health at all.[16] You no longer have the option to "buy" more public health through a reduction in economic activity. Prioritizing the economy too aggressively is like going through a one-way door. There is no exit.

Instead, holding the line on health initially is the superior way to go. It is the only direction that gives you the *option* of making a choice once you have learned more information regarding what the pandemic's effects on your options actually look like. Consequently, from an economics perspective, the fact that supporting the economy makes the decision irreversible by changing the pandemic production options means that you should be biased toward sacrificing the economy and maintaining the line on public health. Thus, our choices are guided by the best way to manage the information problems we face.

Resolve

Based on the above, economics tells us that the optimal response to a pandemic is to resolutely hold the line on health while you consider your options. It is critical to prioritize *health before wealth* until such time as you learn enough information to understand the nature of the pandemic.

Holding the line is a difficult coordination challenge. Expectations matter. To hold the line on health, you need to change the behavior of large numbers of people. It is easy to social distance when others are doing so. It is easy to practice good hygiene when you fear others around you will stigmatize you if you don't. But the flip side of this is that if you cannot achieve that convergence of expectations, you may not be able to achieve significant progress in holding a virus at bay.

In particular, it is important to keep measures in place for long enough for them to have the desired effect. Robert Barro studied the 1918–1919 influenza pandemic in the United States.[17] He found that many of the city-level interventions used to reduce the spread of the infections (such as social distancing, quarantine, and school closures) did not have a large impact on deaths despite reducing the number of infections for a time. He attributes the reason for this lack of impact on the fact that many of those interventions were temporary, with a duration of around a month—too little to have a marked effect on ultimate outcomes according to epidemiologists.

Given this, you might have thought the world's population would have been better prepared to act quickly. However, it is harder than you think, as it requires a faith in mathematical predictions that is not easy to come by.[18] Chapter 3 is about such predictable surprises. It discusses why the mathematics of cumulative processes are so difficult to understand and make decisions on. When we look back on this, I suspect the postmortems will tell us we should have acted sooner. In reality, "sooner" was measured in days. That is a tough standard for decisions that turned out to be vastly consequential.

Technical Interlude

Readers who do not enjoy graphs are free to skip directly to chapter 3 without missing any crucial information. For economists and other graph lovers, this section will go into more detail of the hollowing-out and drift effects so critical to the economic conclusion that health should come before wealth.

The key thing to note about a pandemic (like COVID-19) is that it fundamentally changes the *production possibilities set* for the economy. A production possibilities set tells us what we can produce with the resources at hand. It does not tell us what we should or want to produce; you would need to think about preferences (in this case, social preferences) to get that. Instead, the production possibilities set focuses only on what the economy *can* do, and that is all I need to do to point out the flaws in beliefs that fine-tuning and maintaining the previous balance between health and the economy is possible.

To keep things simple, figure 2.1 is the production possibilities set during "normal" times when we have a choice between how much public health we want and how much of other stuff—which I will label "economy."

The curved black line in figure 2.1 is the production possibilities frontier (PPF) and shows the upper limit of the combinations of the economy and health we can achieve. We can, of course, obtain lower levels of the economy and health than this, but we would try not to. If we can, we want to choose a point (like the dark gray dot) that is on the frontier, which gives us a certain amount of economy and a certain amount of health.

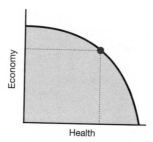

Figure 2.1
Production possibilities set in normal times

The key feature of the textbook PPF is that the shape of the curve is concave. This means that, if you start from a very low level of health and want a bit more, you have to give up only a little bit of economy. However, if you start from a high level of health, to gain even more health, you would need to give up a larger amount of economy. This is the law of diminishing returns. Put simply, it is harder to produce more of something when you already have a lot of it.

These are not normal times. We now have a pandemic. What a pandemic does to the PPF is something like what is depicted in figure 2.2a. There are two big changes illustrated by the new line below the normal PPF. First, the pandemic PPF lies below the normal PPF. That means we can't produce as much economy or health as before. In particular, we can no longer produce to meet the dark gray dot even if we can have the same amount of health or the same amount of economy as before. This is the logic many have when thinking of why we face a trade-off in a pandemic when we didn't before.

Second, there is a hollowing-out of the PPF. That arises out of the nature of a pandemic. To consider this, suppose that we started from our original level of the economy (at a point like E, the black dot). Then, if we want more health during a pandemic, we need to

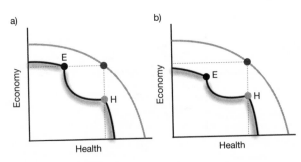

Figure 2.2
Pandemic production possibilities sets. (a) Previous levels possible. (b) Dark recession.

give up a lot of the economy to get it. This is the social distancing argument—we need a lot of social distancing in order to halt the spread of infectious disease, and a little bit won't have much effect. The same logic applies if we start from our original level of health (at a point like H, the light gray dot). In that situation, if we look to give up a little health for a better economy, we find that we cannot do that. Even to achieve a level of health remotely close to what we previously had, we have to employ lots of social distancing, which means that the only way to get a better economy is to give up a great deal of health. (Notice that the less virulent is the infection, the smaller the "bite" is likely to be.) The point is that if we take the epidemiologists seriously, then our usual marginal thinking about trade-offs does not work.[19]

Before moving on, it is useful to reflect on a couple of other things we learn from this approach. First, it is highly unlikely that we want to choose a point in the hollowed-out portion (say, by maintaining the previous balance between health and the economy). Doing this would leave us with lower health or economy than we could achieve at either end.[20]

Second, there is a certain logic to the idea that you might choose to give up entirely on trying to slow or contain a virus and, instead, choose a point like E where you have the economy you had before but with much lower public health (and also fewer people surviving). The logic here is that it is really, really hard to preserve public health because the economy really has to suffer. Of course, the same logic applies to a point like H. If you want to preserve public health (save lives), you have to accept that you will harm the economy in a large way. In other words, the bite forces us into a big either/or situation—that is, a choice between H and E.

Figure 2.2a as it is drawn assumes that we can achieve the same level of economic performance even if we have low public health. That is potentially very unrealistic. If we let a pandemic run its course without mitigation, that lowers economic activity and leads to a "dark recession" as depicted in figure 2.2b. If this is the case, you can see that a point like E will be far less desirable than H.

The drift can also be represented using PPFs. This is done in figure 2.3. Figure 2.3a shows what happens if you do not hold the line on public health to keep it at its previous levels. You will see that option no longer is viable and lies outside the moving pandemic PPF. Figure 2.3b shows what happens if you try to maintain the previous economy level and delay too long on social distancing. In this case, the PPF has a cliff and it is no longer possible to control the pandemic after a time.

There are two final things worth demonstrating using the pandemic PPFs. First, figure 2.4 shows what happens if you hold the line on public health but do not institute the type of macroeconomic policy "life support" mechanisms that allow you to pause the economy. As will be discussed in chapter 6, introducing those mechanisms can improve the economy along with maintaining public health as you move from a point, like B, within the PPF to the frontier itself.

The economist Eric Budish observed that it is very important to consider the correct mindset when thinking about how to reach the frontier.[21] In particular, if you have a mindset that focuses solely on reducing the infection rate as quickly as possible, this will not

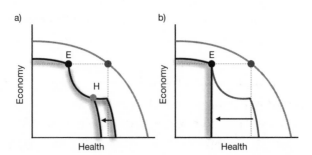

Figure 2.3
The drift. (a) The PPF moves. (b) The cliff.

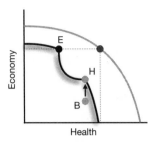

Figure 2.4
Supportive macroeconomic policy.

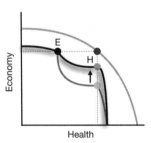

Figure 2.5
Impact of testing.

necessarily get you to the frontier. Instead, that frontier involves targeting an infection rate that stops the pandemic[22] but, otherwise, picking allowable activities that reflect both their value for the economy and their risk in terms of public health.

Second, there are some innovations and investments that can be made that will improve the pandemic PPF. In chapter 7, I describe the use of tests to make interacting physically safe again. This has the effect—shown in figure 2.5—of expanding the production possibilities set. This makes H more desirable. However, it is useful to note that such innovations and investments are of no value if you decide to move to a point like E. Thus, the key reason you may want to hold the line on health is to provide breathing space for the reset phase to be prepared for and then conducted.

Key Points

1. The way in which COVID-19 propagates through the population means that there is a stark choice between maintaining economic activity and public health.

2. Calculations that are designed to weigh the cost to the economy against the cost of health create, at best, a static position, whereas the problem facing policy makers is a dynamic one.

3. If governments choose not to hold the line on public health, there is no going back. The possibilities drift so that the options include worse and worse health outcomes.

4. It is, therefore, economically sensible to prioritize public health during a pandemic in order to learn more about the ways in which the pandemic can be managed.

3

Predictable Surprises

It starts with a grain of rice on a chessboard. This is grain one. The craftsperson makes an offer to the monarch. "I have made this beautiful chessboard and I will give it to you for some more rice. I have placed a grain on the first square. I want you to add grains to each of the remaining squares in turn, doubling each time. Two on the next one. Four on the one after that and so on until all 64 squares have been covered." The monarch feels they can spot a good deal and so accepts the offer.[1]

Suffice it to say, it was not a good deal, and accepting it would surely bankrupt the monarch's land. The reason why it is bad is that it is very clear what is going on, and only a lack of willingness to do the math would allow you to think otherwise. Put simply, the total amount of rice being asked for was not some mystery. It was the solution to this equation:

$$1 + 2 + 4 + \cdots + 9{,}233{,}372{,}036{,}854{,}775{,}808 =$$
$$18{,}446{,}744{,}073{,}709{,}551{,}615$$

That, it turns out, is a lot of rice. If you laid the grains end to end you would go from the Earth to Alpha Centauri and back twice.[2]

Ultimately, there isn't enough rice in the world, let alone the land, to pay out the contract. I'm no lawyer, so I have no idea what the outcome of this would have been had it ended up in the courts.

Obviously, this fable isn't about contract law; it is about our ability to use mathematics to understand the world around us. If you base your decisions on what you can see with little effort, then you might miss the underlying processes at work. Alternatively, if you understand the underlying processes and see them to their ultimate conclusion, you will make a better decision. Those conclusions may be surprising, but, paradoxically, they are predictable.

The COVID-19 pandemic came as a predictable surprise to most people. While the mathematics are not as clear as the rice and the chessboard, they were present, and the same disconnect between what you could see immediately and what the math told you about where this was heading was there. The tough challenge was how to make some potentially very costly decisions based on the mathematics alone.

The Degree of the Problem

Pandemics are better than a rice/chessboard process in a very important way: once the first grain of rice is placed, there are ways to stop the process before square 64 is reached. The key to any mitigation strategy that modifies the mathematics of that process is a willingness make that break.

Before getting to that, it is worthwhile to review the mathematics. When a person contracts an infectious virus, they can pass it to others by contact. This isn't true of all viruses nor of all infectious diseases, but, at the time of writing, this is the most plausible infection path for the novel coronavirus. Sometime in November 2019, someone contracted the virus and began passing it on to others. The question was: How many others? The question pertains not only to that person but, more important, to any random person who might carry the virus.

In epidemiology this has a number, R_0, or the basic reproduction number. R_0 is the expected number of people one infectious person is likely to infect with a particular virus at the outset.[3] In the past, with enough knowledge, R_0 for other viruses or infectious diseases could be measured. Absent any interventions, the critical threshold number is 1. If each infected person infects at most one other person, then the total number of infections might rise initially but will progress very slowly, and, because eventually you are meeting more and more people who have had the virus and are, hopefully, immune, the infection rate will die off fairly quickly. For an $R_0 > 1$, an epidemic is possible, with a much higher share of the population likely to become infected. This is why the initial goal in pandemic management is to create conditions so that the basic reproduction number is moved to less than 1.

The most infectious disease in modern times was measles, with an R_0 between 12 and 18.[4] This is because it could spread in the air. The usual influenza we experience each year is between 0.9 and 2.1. Some years are good, while others are bad. The SARS outbreak was between 2 and 5, while Ebola, which is transmitted via bodily fluids, was between 1.5 and 2.5. You can see both significant variation but also significant ranges of uncertainty. For Ebola, this was likely related to population density. At the time of writing, COVID-19 has an estimated R_0 between 1.4 and 3.9. It is for this reason that many predicted that, left unchecked, 70 percent of all people would eventually contract the virus.

The Human Equation

The interesting thing about R_0 is that it is not just a biological number—that is, related to how a virus can move and bind itself to others—but also a social number.[5] If a hermit contracts the measles, then R_0 is 0. If a partygoer gets it, R_0 is much higher. The estimates of R_0 are averages, which is a guide to decision-making but not what you want to know. In principle, you want to know everyone's specific R_0 and you likely want to draw your attention to reducing the R_0s of those who are at the top of this list.

Rather than individual R_0s, the best we can hope for are group R_0s. For instance, children move about, keep personal hygiene, and live their lives in a very different way from other beings. As any parent with young kids knows, there are years in which your house turns into the town from Albert Camus's *The Plague*, sans any widespread epidemic. This is why, in many countries, the first step in social distancing was to shut down schools. This wasn't because children are especially at risk—they aren't, thank goodness—but because they are "vectors"—an identifiable group known to have potentially high R_0s. The same is true of college students. If most students stayed at college, they were likely to be strong vectors for infection because they spend their days going from numerous gatherings of a hundred people or more before bringing it all back to others in their dorms. By contrast, office workplaces are potentially lower-risk.

The epidemiological models consider who might interact with whom when they try to predict the spread of an infection, but those assumptions are "hard-wired" into their models. Economists (and other social scientists) typically shy away from predictions based on such hard-wired behavior. Instead, when considering how people might interact with one another, they look to their choices. People do not blindly react to pandemics and continue to go about their daily business. Nor do they hide out for the duration. What they do is balance the risk of interactions as the pandemic progresses, based on information they have at hand. In other words, what epidemiological models can miss is that humans change their behavior over time, and this can impact the mathematics of the infection.[6]

The research that integrates economics into epidemiology is very much nascent. However, from the work that has been done to date, some important insights can be drawn. First of all, we can expect that when people are concerned about the costs of being infected, they won't necessarily need to be told to socially distance themselves from others.[7] In particular, as the infection rate starts to climb, more people will reduce their economic activity, which has the effect of moderating the spread of any virus. During the 2009 H1N1 epidemic, people in the United States reduced their time spent among others,[8] and similarly in Mexico, although there the behavior differed among different socioeconomic groups, with poorer groups adjusting less.[9]

Second, it is possible that the behavioral response to a pandemic can cause the peak infection level to be lower than what might otherwise emerge from a standard epidemiological model.[10] This is because, as the infection rate increases, people will perceive greater risk from interacting with others. While that reduces the infection rate, this back and forth (sometimes referred to as "the dance"[11]) will slice the top off the peak but spread the length of the pandemic further; that is, it will "flatten the curve" (discussed in more detail in chapter 5).[12] Consistent with this, examinations of behavior from China and the United States suggested non-mandated social distancing played a significant role only as infections hit their peak but did not have an impact on infection rates at the outset of the COVID-19 epidemic.[13]

This has another important implication that can test our usual epidemic intuition. If a virus is more virulent (that is, can be more easily passed between people), the usual prediction is that a larger share of the population will become infected (as R_0 is relatively high). However, once the human element is taken into account, this could go the other way. If it was known that a virus was particularly virulent, people would fear going out and would socially distance. The more virulent it is, the more people will self-isolate to avoid others. This could well mean that virulent outbreaks have a *lower* total number infected than less virulent ones. This is, of course, just a theoretical possibility at this stage, but there is anecdotal evidence in the COVID-19 outbreak that certain groups—particularly, younger people who have less to fear from the consequences of being infected—do not practice social distancing as much as others.[14]

While people might reduce their social interactions out of fear, it is important to emphasize that this may still be too little relative to what we might all agree would be in the collective interest. That is because people take into account their own fear in refraining from social interactions but not the impact those actions might have on others. This is the textbook definition of an externality—where your own actions have an impact on others that you do not explicitly take into account.[15] At the beginning of an epidemic it can accelerate the rate of infection. At the end, when there is the prospect of the epidemic dying out as sufficient people become immune, individuals have a reason to hold back and let others do the "heavy work" in becoming infected/immune.[16] The upshot is that fear is not necessarily enough, and governments may have to take heavy-handed actions to influence R_0 at different stages of a pandemic.[17]

The good news is that policy actions designed to change the behavior of many can have an impact. This was starkly demonstrated in a comparative study of the Philadelphia and St. Louis responses to the flu pandemic of 1918.[18] As figure 3.1 (drawn from that study) demonstrates, St. Louis had a milder and prolonged epidemic compared with Philadelphia, which had the majority of cases in just one month. The difference between the two was that Philadelphia held a parade of returning soldiers from World War I, while St. Louis, armed with the same health warnings, closed schools and even churches and banned gatherings of more than 20 people. As network economist Matthew Jackson notes, being able to reduce

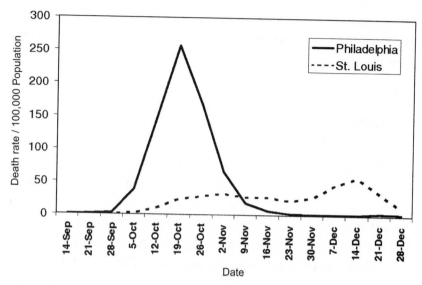

Figure 3.1

Pandemic of 1918. *Source:* Richard J. Hatchett, Carter E. Mecher, and Marc Lipsitch, "Public Health Interventions and Epidemic Intensity during the 1918 Influenza Pandemic," *Proceedings of the National Academy of Sciences* 104, no. 18 (May 2007): 7582–7587 (doi: 10.1073/pnas.0610941104).

the number of highly connected clusters within a network of social relationships can dramatically reduce R_0.[19] An early examination of enforced social distancing policies for COVID-19 suggested that the mix of policy actions taken had dramatically reduced pandemic growth rates, potentially delaying 62 million infections in China, France, the United States, Italy, Iran, and South Korea.[20]

While we understand the general science behind disease transmission, the mix of biological and social factors for each new disease means that we have broad ranges for R_0 and scant details about what any particular measure might do to the spread of the virus. That said, we know that if we shut everything down, then we can minimize any given R_0. In doing so, we maximize the R_0 within a given household, but the idea is to keep the spread between households at a minimum. How much we want to do this depends both on the degree of the problem—how high R_0 would otherwise be—and on the costs of becoming infected versus the costs associated with trying to reduce R_0.

Willingness to Act

This leads us to the costs. The potential health costs of COVID-19 are of primary interest. As I apply my economist filter to what I understand of the biomedical properties here, I see those health costs (in terms of likely medical care) reflected in four groups. The first are the people who contract the virus but have no important symptoms. They create no health costs at all. The second are people who contract the virus and have symptoms akin to a severe flu. The health costs here are primarily in terms of lost ability to work and function. The third are those who have severe enough symptoms to require hospitalization with the obvious associated costs. The final category is those for whom COVID-19 proves to be fatal. Early estimates from China suggested that 81 percent of those who tested positive for COVID-19 were in the first two categories. Of the remainder, 14 percent were severe, and 5 percent were critical. The remaining 2.3 percent had died.[21]

The problem we face is that the mix of people in the third and fourth category potentially depends critically on the ability of the healthcare system to manage their infections and resulting consequences. Economizing on this dimension is the focus of policy makers in minimizing the health costs associated with COVID-19.

There are two ways to achieve this. The first would be to ensure there was sufficient capacity in the healthcare system to handle cases when they are at their most intense. That will be the subject of chapter 5. The second is to reduce the intensity of critical COVID-19 cases at any point in time. In other words, that means taking actions to reduce R_0.

Let's consider ways of reducing R_0 in terms of their costs. The least costly ways are good health practices. This includes thorough hand washing and regular cleaning of surfaces. These are the types of things that occur within hospitals that become of high value during a pandemic. There are also a related set of protocols for the operation of healthcare facilities themselves so as to protect health-care workers. Not surprisingly, these were the first set of measures that were enacted in most countries.

The second set of actions was to limit the spread of the virus across national boundaries. The logic here is that, if the virus has not infected significant numbers of a country's population (and in the case of COVID-19 that would have to be a very small number), then by limiting travel between countries, the virus might be kept out. Some countries, notably Taiwan, did this very quickly, while most others did it in a somewhat ad hoc way. For instance, the United States closed travel to any foreign nationals coming from China but not their own citizens. In March 2020, Israel took the unusual step, at the time, of requiring any person coming in to self-quarantine for two weeks and using cell phones to track infractions. At the time of writing, it is safe to say that the ability to contain the spread across national boundaries was limited. Obviously, restricting travel would start to impact negatively on certain industries, especially tourism, hotels, and airlines.

The third set of actions came under a catchall term of "social distancing." Initially, this involved cancelling large gatherings. In Australia this was 500 people initially, while at a similar time Austria banned gatherings of more than five people (which might have given pause to households with four or more children). This, however, led to more extreme actions such as canceling school and college classes, instituting work-from-home practices, and eventually closing restaurants and bars. Finally, in some jurisdictions there were orders to "shelter in place" (including China, Italy, and parts of the United States).

The first two measures—hygiene and travel restrictions—are disruptive, potentially very disruptive. However, they pale in comparison to the costs associated with social distancing. To achieve social distancing in a manner that would prevent the healthcare system from exceeding capacity requires a reduction in economic activity that would plunge any economy into an immediate recession. This is why there is a reduction in economic activity if you choose to hold the line on health. How to handle that is the subject of chapter 6. Nonetheless, however you cut it, the costs are significant, perhaps of the order of 10 to 20 percent of GDP of any country. And this is just the economic cost. You are also asking much of the population to remain at home. Thanks to the internet, in many places it has never been more comfortable to do this. Nonetheless, it is unknown just how long such social distancing can last.

So herein lies the basic trade-off. We want to reduce R_0, as it is very costly to have a high number of sick people at one time. The reason we have to do this is because of the limited healthcare system capacity. If R_0 is too high, healthcare capacity becomes quickly overwhelmed and doctors have to engage in triage, which in the context of COVID-19 often means choosing who will live and who will die. This outcome has to be balanced against the significant economic cost associated with spreading infections over time. To be effective, social distancing has to go the distance. But with every week or month of low economic activity, the costs rise.

If that weren't a tough enough trade-off, it is actually worse than that. Whether or not people can develop immunity from COVID-19 is still an open scientific question, but let's assume that it is more likely to be true than not. If you reduce R_0 too far, initially, then most of the population does not become infected and that means that once you stop policies such as social distancing, the virus can emerge once more, and we all have to do this again. It is a reasonable assumption that we want to intervene only once.

The reason there is a cost to this is that you are actually more socially useful if you get the virus and recover and thus are no longer a possible carrier. That means that other people and society do not have to fear interactions with you. In other words, achieving "herd immunity" is an investment in the future. It is like a vaccine, but, alas, you have to actually get the virus rather than an injection. For an understandably short time, the British response to the pandemic, reflecting this idea, was to embrace the idea of "taking one for the team." That said, a week in bed is one thing; dying is another. How you conduct this policy without getting significant people in the latter category is hard to see.

How Will I Know?

Thus, governments face a real quandary: When should social distancing be instituted and how intensive should it be? The problem is that there is uncertainty.[22] If a virus has a low R_0, you need not undertake extreme social distancing measures quickly. On the other hand, if R_0 is high, actions need to be taken. If those infected by COVID-19 could be readily identified—à la our red nose example in chapter 1—then it is likely that the components of R_0—how many people one infected person transmits the virus to and how long they are infectious—can be known fairly quickly, and appropriate containment policies can be chosen quickly as well. The same is true for how severe the virus's effects are on health. If these are severe, the case for fast and intensive action is raised, as they were for Ebola. If these are not severe, few actions are taken—as they often are for, say, annual flu seasons.

You do not necessarily need a big red nose to identify R_0. If there are clear symptoms, these can convey the same information. The problem with COVID-19 is that many of the initial symptoms—fever, cough, breathing issues—were also symptoms of influenza and the common cold. Thus, a clearer test is needed. These diagnostic tests involve taking a swab from deep in the nasal cavity and testing the resulting material for the genetic markers of the novel coronavirus. More recent tests are able to determine this from saliva. These can tell you whether someone is infected or not.

However, in addition to knowing who is infected, you also need broader surveillance information—that is, what proportion of the population has been infected at a given time and how is this changing over time. Using that information, you can estimate R_0. The problem was that in many countries, tests were costly and, in some cases, not available in large enough numbers. Hence, they were used to diagnose those who already had symptoms. This would be fine if all infected people presented symptoms, but for COVID-19, it appeared that many infectious people were either asymptomatic (never got any symptoms) or pre-symptomatic (were infectious before symptoms emerged). In other words, by testing just the symptomatic, you were likely to be dramatically underestimating the total share of people who were infected. And without that information, you did not have real information on R_0.[23]

The obvious way to overcome that difficulty was to engage in broader testing of the population without regard to whether someone had symptoms or not. Such randomized testing of a large enough sample of the population could identify the infection rate. Doing it repeatedly could measure how fast the infection was spreading. This would also allow you to understand precisely how many people may be asymptomatic, which, in many respects, is the primary information gap needed to take appropriate action.[24] Indications from the US carrier *Theodore Roosevelt*, which tested their entire crew, found that 60 percent of carriers were asymptomatic, and in Iceland, where 6 percent of the population were tested, 43 percent were asymptomatic.[25] Given that the test itself often failed to identify a positive coronavirus carrier, this suggested that the likely share of infected was higher than expected. This will be confirmed only if a test for coronavirus antibodies of sufficient accuracy is developed and then undertaken. What this meant was that at the time governments needed to make decisions to intervene to stop the spread of COVID-19, key information was lacking.

The information gap is exacerbated because we know that time can be of the essence.[26] For COVID-19, wait a day to act and you might have 40 percent more cases 21 days later than if you acted immediately.[27] As time goes on, that 40 percent becomes a very large number. The more limited your information, the harder it is to act and achieve results. So, for a country where the outbreak commences, choosing when to socially distance is a very difficult choice. Moreover, given that today's travel possibilities can lead to transmission out of a country very quickly, placing the onus of that decision on the country of origin may not be enough. In the case of COVID-19, it was more than a month before China started to impose travel restrictions.[28] In retrospect, the price to be paid by the world was very high. However, what we were asking China to do was to pay a price themselves. These types of decisions are rarely pursued optimally. Moreover, for countries that could observe outbreaks elsewhere and failed to act quickly, even in terms of their own self-interest, excuses could run out. That said, at the time of writing, it was still unknown why some places, like the Dominican Republic, had outbreaks, while others, like neighboring Haiti, did not.[29]

The point of this is to demonstrate just how hard it is to pull the trigger on measures to reduce R_0 when an outbreak has just begun. There is uncertainty, and, moreover, the costs of actions are felt disproportionately. However, the notion that delaying a day or two will have much in the way of real benefits is a false comfort. If you choose to shut down your economy on Wednesday rather than Tuesday, a day's work and economic activity is lost. But that is peanuts relative to the costs associated with a shutdown at all. The takeaway, therefore, is that if you *know* you are going to shut down the country eventually, there are huge returns to doing it quickly.[30]

One reason to delay is to gather more information. If you will learn by Wednesday that you could safely keep schools open, you might do well to continue to keep them open on Tuesday. What is more, it may be that shutting down early causes you to miss that critical information altogether. Thus, while "the drift" told us that if we do not hold the line on health, we may take away options we could use, it is nonetheless true that we can learn about different ways of containing the virus based on the actions we take.[31] Indeed, if an aggressive lockdown is pursued, it may not be conceptually possible to learn the non-lockdown value of R_0 at all. That said, because essential services keep operating, there is scope to use those sectors of the population to learn about the infectiousness of a virus.

Delaying a decision in order to gather more information has a value in economics called the *real option value*. This is a concept we previous alluded to when discussing "the drift" in chapter 2. Let's consider it in more detail. Suppose you need to consider when to shut down the economy for a month or more. You know that will have potential costs, but those costs are like an investment in terms of the benefits associated with reducing R_0. The decision to shut down will be the same on Tuesday versus Wednesday unless you learn something in the interim. Suppose you are predisposed to shut down on Tuesday, but there is more information to be accumulated.[32] Should you wait?

It turns out the answer depends on the type of information you are expecting to receive. As noted by Ben Bernanke, chair of the Federal Reserve during the 2008 financial crisis, if you are expecting news that will justify and reinforce the decision you were already predisposed to make on Tuesday, there is no reason to wait.[33] That information will not change your mind. Instead, the reason to wait is if you receive news that will convince you not to shut down. *The only information that gives you an option value of waiting to pull the trigger is news that would cause you to remove your finger from the trigger entirely.*[34]

As I write this, it is hard to imagine the information governments were expecting to receive that would have caused them *not* to act on some type of social distancing. If there was hope, it was not articulated nor in the data. Thus, we are left to speculate. My speculation is that waiting was driven by receiving political news rather than scientific or economic news.[35] Governments may have decided not to shut down if they found that a large proportion of the population would resist those efforts. In many cases, this is why governments implored citizens to engage in social distancing in the hope that they could achieve a reduction in R_0 without stronger measures. Those stronger measures included legal requirements to stay at home, which could potentially then be enforced with penalties associated with violations.

In summary, it is important to realize that acting decisively is very challenging. It is more challenging depending on the style of government, the transparency of information, and the competence of the decision makers. In the end, most governments eventually made strong moves to reduce R_0, and they did so in a manner that, on reflection, was relatively fast compared with decisions of far less consequence. In retrospect, with situations like this, we may always conclude that governments should have acted earlier. The important question for the future is: How can we change our information-gathering processes so that information gaps are closed and knowledge is transmitted to those who need to make key decisions?

Key Points

1. The mathematics of pandemics means that when the basic reproduction number (R_0) is greater than one, the outbreak will not naturally end until a large fraction of the population has immunity.

2. The exponential properties associated with infectious outbreaks, like COVID-19, mean that delay in actions—such as social distancing and identifying who is infected and isolating them—can be very costly in terms of much higher numbers of infections.

3. People will, if given the information, engage in some social distancing in order to mitigate their own risk of infection. However, in making those choices, they neglect the impact they may have on others becoming infected. Thus, governments need to act to ensure that such practices actually take place at a sufficient level.

4. The timing of when to act is a very difficult decision because, in the case of a pandemic, many of its properties are not known at the outset, while the costs of suppression are very high.

4

Telling the Truth

This is one I fell for. In early March, I told my colleagues, with a passion, that it was stupid to wear a face mask when traveling. This was an opinion I had come to having read government statements and media reports. This was also the clear statement from the US Surgeon General:

> Seriously people—STOP BUYING MASKS!
>   They are NOT effective in preventing general public from catching #Coronavirus, but if healthcare providers can't get them to care for sick patients, it puts them and our communities at risk![1]

The clearest of these was from the World Health Organization (WHO), which recommended that masks be worn only by those who were sick. Even by late March, their line, as stated by Mike Ryan, Executive Director of WHO health emergencies program, was:

> There is no specific evidence to suggest that the wearing of masks by the mass population has any potential benefit. In fact, there's some evidence to suggest the opposite in the misuse of wearing a mask properly or fitting it properly.[2]

The rationale was that only certain masks (such as the N95) could protect the wearer from the coronavirus, which was small enough that it would pass through surgical or cloth masks. There was a shortage of all masks, and, thus, the limited supply needed to be preserved for healthcare workers. That made sense to me. If the masks weren't necessary, then what you didn't want was people hoarding them for no good reason. When I passed mask wearers on the street, I thought that they were selfish morons.

Things, however, did not add up. In East Asian countries where mask wearing when sick was considered socially responsible, the outbreak seemed to be more contained. While one could point to other explanations, it did stand out that Taiwan, Hong Kong, South Korea, and Japan all seemed to be doing better without harsh social distancing rules in place and widespread mask use (with a daily growth rate of infections of 10 percent rather than 18 percent elsewhere).[3] Moreover, given that asymptomatic people might be infectious[4] and past and increasing evidence that mask wearing did prevent the spread of the virus from the wearer to others,[5] there was a likely mechanism that supported widespread mask wearing as a public health policy.[6] Economists estimated that every additional mask wearer might contribute $3,000 to $6,000 in public health benefits. In many countries, the advice changed to recommend (e.g., in the United States just five weeks after the statements referenced earlier[7]) and, in some cases, to require the wearing of masks. Airlines signaled that mask wearing would be mandated. My family, however, having heeded earlier advice, did not have any masks, and, by that time, they were hard to come by.

We, the public, were played. And we were played by those whom we were supposed to trust implicitly because of their expertise.[8] And I played a role in trying to spread that advice to my colleagues, who ignored me and bought some masks just in case (including an extra one or two for me).

Let's unpack this. Was there a mask shortage? Yes, there was. Should healthcare workers be prioritized to receive those masks? Yes, they should. Did surgical and cloth masks completely protect the wearer? They did not. Thus, technically, no one had lied to the public on that basis. But health officials did have a goal, which was to prevent people buying up masks. And some, like Mike Ryan of the WHO and Jerome Adams, the US Surgeon General, as evidenced in the statements above, chose to get to that goal by telling people that masks had no health value. That last step was the falsehood.[9] Masks did not necessarily protect the wearer but could be very useful in protecting others from the wearer. A better policy message would have been to prioritize healthcare workers for existing masks, and to ensure the creation of new masks to help curtail the spread of the virus outside the home.[10]

The problem with the misinformation is that it cut off, or at least made very difficult, the second goal of mask wearing to protect others. First of all, by saying for a month and a half that masks were of no value, market forces could not come into play. Making acceptable cloth masks is within the scope of the economy, especially with otherwise idle resources, but that didn't happen right away. Second, people do not want to wear masks. A good way to motivate them is if there is some value for them as protection. As it turns out, while they are not 100 percent effective, there is some protective value to wearing a mask.[11] That information, however, is now distorted and not necessarily persuasive. Third, the more protective masks, such as the N95, can have valves that filter air coming in but not air coming out, which means that they won't perform a socially beneficial function. In other words, you want people to wear masks potentially less protective of them than of others. Finally, in order to get people to wear masks for social reasons—to prevent the spread to others—you likely cannot rely on soft persuasion but, instead, need to have more strictly enforced policies. This is more expensive and also fosters discontent. Although, as the Czech Republic demonstrates, a mandate early enough did have positive effects.[12] As we face a situation where masks will need to be worn for a year or two, distrust is a constraint that likely would really undermine public health pushes.

No critique of actions like this should be judged without considering the counterfactual—What should have been done, especially given that there were real issues of the supply of medical-grade masks? Sociologist Zeynep Tufekci, who has studied misinformation, believed that telling the nuanced and unvarnished truth would be superior:

> If anything, a call for people who hoarded masks to donate some of them to their local medical workers would probably work better than telling people that they don't need them or that they won't manage to make them work. "Look, more masks would be great. We are doing our best to ramp up production. Till then, if our medical workers fall ill, we will all be worse off. Please donate any excess— maybe more than two weeks' worth per person—to your hospital" sounds corny, but it's the truth. Two weeks is a reasonable standard because the C.D.C. and the W.H.O. still recommend wearing masks if you're taking care of someone with a milder illness self-isolating at home, something that will increasingly be necessary as hospitals get overwhelmed.[13]

This, she argues, would have appealed to people's altruism, and had the officials communicated that truth it would have been done while they still possessed default trust. This could have been supplemented by other information, such as the app the Taiwanese government made available that showed people the stocks of masks available in nearby stores.[14] Doing this would have avoided causing a leak in what epidemiologist Carl Bergstrom called the "reservoir of trust" that many health experts start out with.[15] Moreover, with respect to the potential scarce supply, if masks had been seen as important, this statement could have allowed a more proactive and obvious move to manufacture these for the entire population, something which Taiwan moved to do at the onset of the crisis.

Given this clear example, this chapter will examine, in more detail, the value of trust in managing crises like COVID-19 and how misinformation can not only undermine that trust but also cause actions that are not in the interests of good public health management.[16] How can leaders be persuasive at times like this while at the same time not stoking behaviors whereby citizens are moved to pursue their private interests above what is socially desirable (such as personal hoarding of masks)? Here is where the pandemic information problem morphs beyond what the key decision makers know to what is generally known and understood. As we will see later in this chapter, perhaps there are circumstances when misinformation can be justified, although we'll come to understand why this particular obfuscation ultimately does not serve the greater good.

The Art of Persuasion

The issue with communication is that it causes the recipients to act in a certain way. If you do not want people to panic in a crowded theater, you do not call out "fire" whether there is a fire or not as it could create a panic. This poses an issue. You want people to clear out of a theater if there is, in fact, a fire but not in a way that causes more damage or is counterproductive. What you would like is for people to file out in an orderly way. If your *only* choices are to shout "fire" or not, you may not be able to achieve that by just telling the truth. If your message is always the truth, then when there is actually a fire, people will run for the door and not otherwise. On the other hand, suppose that, if there is a fire you let people know, but, sometimes, even if there isn't one, you say there is a fire. If people understand this rule, then even when there is a fire and you let people know, some people won't be so sure and will not be as quick to leave their seats. The trick will be to ensure they eventually leave. You could be forgiven for thinking whether people would really shout "fire" when there isn't one. But then consider how often smoke detectors go off or fire alarms are activated even when there is no smoke. And then consider how quickly you reacted. The point is that having a little doubt about the seriousness of the situation in this case can get people to have a more relaxed exit but hopefully not cause people to ignore it entirely. Managing exit when panic is possible requires some nuanced messaging.

Notice this all works because there are times you believe that you are not being told accurate information. But it also is necessary because people will act in their own interests even when such actions have a negative impact on others. In the case of the theater, your desire to rush to the door impedes others and vice versa. In other words, if it was just you in the theater, there would be value to transparent truth-telling, but because it is you and others, there is value to obfuscation to get everyone to behave better. Not surprisingly, in a pandemic, what communication impacts is not only your own beliefs and actions but those of others. Experts might see as their best option, in certain situations, to sometimes obscure the unvarnished truth.

Which brings me back to masks. Masks have a theater-fire aspect in that when there is a pandemic, we want people to wear them but not to hoard them—the equivalent of leaving the theater in an orderly fashion—even if they find it costly to do so—that is, they would rather flee. Thus, if your goal is to stop people from rushing to hoard masks, then even if there is a pandemic, you want to downplay the need to wear masks, as the WHO Executive Director and US Surgeon General did. If the only messages you can effectively send is whether there is a pandemic or not, then you might sometimes say there is no pandemic when there actually is one.

But what if, absent information to the contrary, people did not want to wear masks? (This is reasonable because, if they wanted to wear them all of the time, this whole communication problem wouldn't exist.) This means that, in order to persuade people to wear masks when it is definitely socially beneficial to do so, we need to sometimes tell them to wear masks when that is not the case—that is, when the experts believe that an outbreak is not as serious.

In this situation, if the experts say the pandemic is not serious, people will definitely not wear a mask. But if they say that it is serious, people may not be sure, but this raises the probability they think it is serious by just enough so that they choose to wear a mask rather than take the risk.[17]

Hopefully you can see the issue here compared with the situation we found ourselves in for COVID-19. With COVID-19, experts told the public that the situation was not serious enough for them to wear masks in order to discourage mask wearing. As the public was not predisposed to wear or buy masks, this was a clear signal for them not to do that. Thus, they did not wear them. But when the experts switched course and said it was actually serious enough, then people were not sure what to believe. The experts had not learned any new information but had decided that they wanted to encourage rather than discourage mask wearing. As a result of this about-face, however, the authorities are going to struggle to convince people to wear masks. If people are reluctant to wear masks, you want to tell them not to wear masks only when they clearly should not wear masks and be encouraging otherwise. Instead, health officials in the United States initially presented a clear picture that mask wearing conferred no health benefits. This undermined their ability to later persuade an otherwise reluctant population to action.[18]

When people do not trust the information they are receiving, they will adjust their behavior. Sometimes that can work well. But if the signal is completely distorted, then you lose the power to persuade. As Tufekci writes:

> providing top-down guidance with such obvious contradictions backfires exactly because lack of trust is what fuels hoarding and misinformation. It used to be said that back in the Soviet Union, if there was a line, you first got in line and then figured out what the line was for—people knew that there were going to be shortages and that the authorities often lied, so they hoarded. And when people feel as though they may not be getting the full truth from the authorities, snake-oil sellers and price gougers have an easier time.[19]

Thus, it is not simply guidance on masks that becomes a problem but guidance on other things. It prevents the authorities from being persuasive when they need to be and also when they need to simply provide people with information to help them navigate the crisis.

If your ability to be persuasive breaks down, the only alternative to get people to undertake the actions you want is to use authority. As already noted, this is likely to be used with respect to the wearing of face masks in many places. However, if people do not believe in the rationale behind wearing face masks, this means resources will need to be devoted to enforcement to ensure compliance. Put simply, even if you are using authority to ensure an outcome, being persuasive can be useful as it makes compliance cheaper.[20]

Wearing face masks is a somewhat straightforward policy which masks (!) the benefits from being persuasive. If economies are going to be partially reopened with a less extreme form of social distancing, this will work well if individuals understand the risks associated with physical interactions more clearly. What you don't want, for instance, is for people to be told it is unsafe to leave their homes under any circumstances. The following is from economist Emily Oster:

> For about two months now, Americans have been told the same thing over and over again by public-health officials and influencers everywhere: Stay home to stop the spread of the coronavirus.
>
> The message is true. If we all stay hermetically sealed in our homes for long enough, the virus will die out; if we don't, it will linger. But framing the message in such a stark way may inadvertently encourage people to make worse choices. A less extreme, more nuanced, set of recommendations may get more traction—perhaps a public-health equivalent of "Reduce, reuse, recycle." Something like "Stay close to home, keep your distance, wash your hands," but catchier. . . .
>
> Stark messaging may also discourage people from taking reasonable precautions. Public-health officials tell people to wash their hands and wear masks. But because the above-the-fold message is "Just stay home," people may struggle to understand the purpose of these other pieces of advice. *If the only truly safe thing to*

do is stay home, then how should I think about the mask suggestion? Is it
a futile gesture, like putting a Band-Aid on a gunshot wound?[21]

Instead, you want to ensure that the public understands the virus and give them ways of assessing risks to take appropriate actions, for instance, who to avoid, what places might lead to the virus spreading, why hand washing matters, and so on.

This type of change in behavior has happened before. During the AIDS epidemic, new patterns of protection needed to be adopted to prevent sexual transmission of the underlying HIV virus. There was no real scope to use authority in this situation, and, instead, it was only through awareness of risks that people could be persuaded to change their behavior. In other words, when individual circumstances matter and there is a need for individual effort as a part of health interventions, then there is no substitute for persuasion.[22] Thus, it is critically important that when risks are communicated, especially when those risks are changing as new information comes to light, that individuals remain cautious and that authorities preserve their reservoir of trust so that when they tell people to feel safe, people do.[23]

Controlling Infodemics

A trusted source for information serves another critical function: it can prevent bad information from filling the vacuum. When there is a high degree of uncertainty, another aspect of the information problem is that misinformation can spread through society like—and this is no accidental naming—a virus. This situation has been given a name: *infodemics*.[24]

Infodemics are sometimes misinformation, such as where a virus initially came from. The 1918 pandemic was referred to as the "Spanish Flu," which gives people the impression that the virus originated in Spain. There is, in fact, no evidence to suggest that.

Instead, the name arose when the flu spread to Spain and the press reported cases including the notable one of King Alfonso XIII. This gave a widespread impression that Spain was the root of the outbreak and had more cases than elsewhere. Today, the practice has become to not name viruses after places, which is why the novel coronavirus has the simple name SARS-CoV-2.

The immediate issue arises when misinformation leads to actions that have detrimental health consequences. In some cases, misinformation causes people to take more health risks than they should. For instance, there are continuing beliefs that there is a link between vaccinations and autism in children. The origin of this particular infodemic came from an otherwise trusted source, an article in *The Lancet* that found a link between autism and the MMR vaccine. Since autism diagnoses were on the rise, there was uncertainty, and, for many, the vaccination link was plausible. However, the study was flawed (based on just 12 children) and the article was misread as being causal. The lead researcher had also received funding from a conflicted source, and this had not been disclosed. Finally, it turned out the sparse data itself were inaccurate. *The Lancet* eventually retracted the article, but the damage had been done. The MMR vaccine rate dropped from 90 to 80 percent the year it was published.[25] Measles outbreaks continue to this day despite a large volume of studies showing no link between vaccines and autism.

The same issue has arisen with respect to COVID-19. Different governments and media outlets have conveyed health risks in different ways. One study noted that on the Fox News Network, in February 2020, the Hannity program was dismissive of COVID-19 risks, while the Carlson program, an hour earlier, was not. In January, both had been similar in their dismissal of health risks, and by March the tone of the two programs had once again come closer together to emphasize health risks. In a careful study, but not peer reviewed as of the time of this writing, economists exploited these changes in tone along with differential viewership numbers across the United

States for these two programs to see if the different messaging had a health impact.[26] They found that in areas with higher relative viewership of Hannity to Carlson, there were 30 percent more COVID-19 cases on March 14 and 21 percent more deaths on March 28. After mid-March, the relative differences declined. This study complemented other studies that showed different rates of concern for the coronavirus among Republican and Democrat voters in the United States with the plausible explanation being the fact that Republican politicians were more likely to dismiss COVID-19 risks than Democrats.[27] What this shows is that information received by individuals from sources they trust does potentially have an impact on beliefs and, indeed, how they confront health risks.[28]

Both the autism/vaccine and the COVID-19 infodemics show that the outset of the spread of misinformation can well be messages from a source that is trusted by those who initially believe what they are being told. In other words, infodemics spread because, once those messages are demonstrated to be false, they cannot easily be dislodged. This is because they tend to build upon one another. A rumor has a different meaning if you have heard it before—perhaps because it spread unchecked quickly—than if you have not.[29] The latter confers skepticism precisely because it seems implausible that you did not hear it sooner. Sadly, that same skepticism can make it difficult to dislodge misinformation once it has been going around.

What can increase the spread of misinformation is when actions are not simply about personal health risk but cause people to hoard various products they believe they might need to mitigate health risks. This was the concern that officials had with regard to face masks that led to the problems outlined earlier. But in pandemics it also arises with respect to purported treatments or cures. Some of these may simply be dangerous, while others may be innocuous, and the harm is where they are hoarded when their use is required elsewhere. This was the case with the malaria treatment hydroxychloroquine, which was hypothesized to be effective against COVID-19. In the absence of any conclusive evidence of its efficacy, it was used and hoarded, which made supplies scarce for its standard use in treating lupus and arthritis. When there is unresolved uncertainty, individuals can take actions that may well harm others indirectly. Once again, this is where officials having a reservoir of trust can play a key role in mitigating the spread of such information.[30]

Managing the information problem in a pandemic requires not just reducing uncertainty but also ensuring that uncertainty is not falsely resolved.

Key Points

1. Public officials often try to use stark messaging to convey recommendations to the public and get them to move in a certain direction. However, when the basis for that message turns out to be false, this can make it difficult to change course.

2. Persuasion requires being very clear when you tell people to refrain from an action they do not want to do (such as wear masks). Otherwise, when you want them to take such actions, they will be harder to convince regarding the underlying risks that motivate the desired outcome.

3. Authorities have a reservoir of trust that can be drawn down. If this happens, then they may be forced to use coercion rather than persuasion to achieve health outcomes.

4. In the absence of trusted sources of information, people may start to believe falsehoods and spread those falsehoods to one another. This can impede proper health messaging.

5

A War Footing

"It is not easy for a free community to organize for war," wrote John Maynard Keynes in 1940.[1] He was commenting on something very obvious: people do not like to be told what to do. Keynes was frustrated by the inability of political leaders to lucidly explain to the public what needed to be done. Resources had to be allocated to the war effort, and, after that, a clear statement of how the remainder would be shared among the public had to be made. Instead, politicians were glossing over both issues with superlatives and no clear plan. At the early stages of the crisis, as politicians announced one day what they claimed was unthinkable the day before, it was easy to understand where Keynes is coming from even if the magnitude of the problem seems comfortably lower.

Keynes was particularly concerned that the decisions that needed to be made were numerous and interrelated with one another.

> Is it better that the War Office should have a large reserve of uniforms in stock or that the cloth should be exported to increase the Treasury's reserve of foreign currency? Is it better to employ our shipyards to build warships or merchant-men? Is it better that a

20-year-old agricultural worker should be left on the farm or taken into the army?

He pointed out the obvious. A start was to think about which margin to fix—the standard of civilian life or the war effort—leaving the other as the residual. This had to be decided one way or the other. As discussed in chapter 2, we faced the same stark choice for the COVID-19 crisis. In the end, many appeared to agree that we should fight the pandemic first and adjust the rest. But looking at the fact that, in 1940, Keynes was pointing out that it was not obvious what Britain had decided should lead us to understand that debates about priorities in crises are hardly new.

It is for this reason that having a clear and resolved approach to holding the line on health is warranted. With a clear resolve to place public health first, we end up at a point where we have the opportunity to improve public health without as much of a sacrifice to the economy. But when political leaders give in to the temptation to try to achieve both too early, they have failed to contain the virus and, thus, have chosen a lower point with regard to public health.[2] That situation calls for strong measures to move back to what might be possible.

It is a striking fact that even the most market-loving, capitalist nations quickly abandoned the decentralized process of allocating resources in the face of World War II. No one expected the military to use markets to decide where to deploy troops and equipment, but the fact that the rest of the economy moved to a war footing in this way is useful to reflect on. In particular, for the most part, even though they may have flirted for a day with relying on strong advice to citizens, governments in the COVID-19 pandemic realized that was insufficient to their ends and ended up with strict and, in some cases, very strictly enforced policies. More authoritarian regimes were a little quicker to act initially, but the lag could be measured in days for most countries.

Why Central Coordination?

Economists claim that markets are the most efficient way of allocating resources and solving the age-old problem of who gets what if there isn't enough to go around. Markets are quite amazing in this regard, and every economist has their moment of wonder that markets work. The following is by Thomas Schelling:

> Most people, whether they drive their own taxis or manage continent-wide airlines, are expected to know very little about the whole economy and the way it works. They know the prices of the things they buy and sell, the interest rates at which they lend and borrow, and something about the pertinent alternatives to the ways they are currently earning their living or running their business or spending their money. The dairy farmer doesn't need to know how many people eat butter and how far away they are, how many other people raise cows, how many babies drink milk, or whether more money is spent on beer than on milk. What he needs to know is the prices of different feeds, the characteristics of different cows, the different prices farmers are getting for milk according to its butter fat content, the relative costs of hired labor and electrical machinery, and what his net earnings might be if he sold his cows and raised pigs instead or sold his farm and took the best job for which he's qualified in some city he is willing to live in.
>
> Somehow all of the activities seem to get coordinated. There's a taxi to get you to the airport. There's butter and cheese for lunch on the airplane. There are refineries to make the airplane fuel and trucks to transport it, cement for the runways, electricity for the escalators, and, most important of all, passengers who want to fly where the airplanes are going.[3]

It is a miracle and we should appreciate it as such. The problem is that it doesn't always get the job done.

When the job to be done is urgent and resources need to be reallocated quickly, the system can gum up. The issue is not markets per se but the problems of relying on a decentralized process whereby everyone allocates the resources they control on the basis of their own information and preferences. Indeed, the problem we face in a time of war (or pandemic) is that resources, currently controlled by individuals, all need to be applied to a new end, and the task of convincing everyone to choose to do so is unlikely to work out well.

This notion was captured in a 1990 paper by economists Patrick Bolton and Joe Farrell.[4] Imagine a situation where we need one factory to produce face masks and another to produce ventilators, but we don't know which will be able to do each task at the lowest cost. In a market economy, each factory owner might look at the situation and try to work out what to do. One option is that they both jump in and start producing the product they think they will provide most efficiently. They retool for that purpose, but there is a chance that they will end up both choosing the same thing and we will end up with too many face masks and too few ventilators or vice versa. Another option is to wait and see what the other factory chooses to do and then do the opposite. But in this world, we have both factories waiting to see what happens and there is a consequent delay. In other words, decentralization either will not get the job done or will cause it to be delayed.

The alternative is for someone to choose who does what. This is the role of central coordination. This prevents both duplication and delay but opens up another problem: the government may make the wrong choice. The factories may end up producing both goods at a higher cost than otherwise. At times of crisis, however, we do not let the perfect be the enemy of the good and so comfortably resort to centralized resource allocation and bear the potential productive inefficiency.[5]

There are three areas where, in the COVID-19 pandemic, market processes have been abandoned in favor of centralized coordination and control. These include the mobilization of resources to dramatically expand healthcare system capacity, the institution of price controls for certain important goods and services, and the use of blanket restrictions on movement of people. Each of these will be discussed in turn.

Surfing the Curve

The initial responses from governments to the pandemic were to institute progressively strong forms of social distancing in the hope of reducing R_0 (the number of people infected people themselves infect). Those responses had the goal of what came to be known as "flattening the curve." In a scenario where this needs to be done once, this involved a scenario such as depicted in figure 5.1. The task was not so much to reduce the total number who became infected but to spread them out over time to economize on health-care system resources.

The problem is determining how flat we need to go. The flatter the goal, the harder it is to achieve and, moreover, the greater are the consequent costs of prolonged economic harm, social isolation,

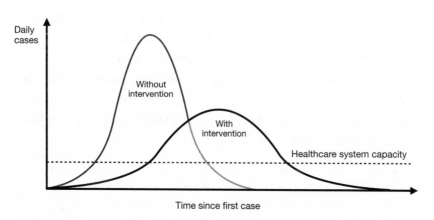

Figure 5.1
Flattening the curve.

and the possibilities that there could be a subsequent reemergence of the pandemic, causing us to do it over again.[6]

The healthcare system capacity is likely much lower than the diagram is showing beyond what flattening the curve can actually achieve. This differs by country. Japan has 13 beds per 1,000 people, while the United States has fewer than three beds per 1,000. And this is just one statistic. There are large national differences in key inputs such as ICU beds, ventilators, hospital protective equipment, and healthcare workers. Nonetheless, in most cases, it is clear that policies aimed at reducing R_0 have happened too late to prevent healthcare system capacity from being reached. In Italy, doctors are having to make heart-breaking triage decisions to determine which patients would get scarce resources. From an economics perspective, the demand on healthcare resources was going to far outstrip supply. What is more, there was no prospect or desire to use higher prices to deal with the shortage. As Keynes noted for World War II, a plan for rationing was required, but no plan was being formulated.

Given this, a massive expansion in healthcare capacity was required.

While flattening the curve can take place and reduce the required capacity expansion, what is required is to surf the curve (see figure 5.2). In this situation, healthcare system capacity would be temporarily expanded so as to cover the unflattened portion of the curve.

Building out that capacity requires a new mindset and requires it quickly. The nature of the problem was obvious on the ground. The following are the words of Dr. Daniel Horn (a physician at Massachusetts General Hospital in Boston):

> In the face of a global shortage, American industries can step up and quickly produce ventilators. All week, I have been receiving text messages and emails that say things like "By the way, my company makes parts for G.E. ventilators. We just got a big order that we are pushing through as fast as we can." The General Motors chief executive, Mary T. Barra, announced that G.M. was working closely with Ventec Life Systems, one of a few ventilator companies

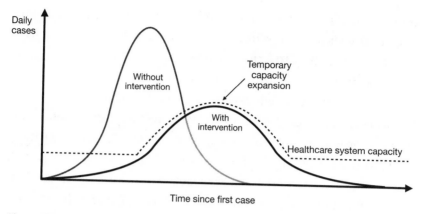

Figure 5.2
Surfing the curve.

based in the U.S., to rapidly scale up production of their critically important respiratory products. My colleagues at the nation's top hospitals are getting phone calls from tech leaders asking for ventilator specs.

Such stories give me hope. But we need the federal government, too. . . . We need a plan.[7]

Sound familiar? This is precisely the coordination problem as outlined by Bolton and Farrell. Hospitals alone cannot procure what they need. Some factories can make some parts better than others. And then there is the issue of which hospitals to send them to. There has been little information present, and, in the United States, despite having the powers to do so, no central action has been taken.

This has highlighted the need for a war-like resource allocation mindset. Someone is needed to take control, and, when it came to fast and rapid capacity of healthcare, most countries have an obvious candidate: the military. Mobile Army Surgical Hospitals (MASH), as portrayed in the TV show, are a part of the armed forces; they just had to be moved to civilian ends. In some countries, this happened with the military preparing and/or building facilities, for example, in Switzerland, Colombia, the Netherlands, Italy, and France. The United States has also redirected hospital ships to California and New York to handle patients with other conditions who might be pushed out of those systems.

The numbers involved, however, suggest that a more comprehensive and aggressive solution is likely to be required: not only military provision but also a means of diverting manufacturing effort to the cause. Much of this has been lying idle due to social distancing. The need is for a centralized process to unlock that potential and ensure timely provision. In World War II, businesses quickly retooled for military production. The same was required in this crisis.

In the end, the experience in Italy moved other countries to action.[8] In regions where outbreaks were concentrated (like New York City), new hospital capacity was added, and the military was called in to assist with the expansion. This mirrored action taken by China earlier in Wuhan, building entirely new hospitals in just over a week. At the beginning of March 2020, healthcare industry insiders thought that such expansions were not possible. They were used to working within constraints. However, it turned out that policies to flatten the curve accompanied by capacity expansion prevented persistent shortages. This would not have happened without government capacity to take charge.

Price Controls

Hand sanitizer and toilet paper went first. Hand sanitizer made sense. It was a genuine surge in demand as people expected to use more, much more, of it and were advised to do so. Toilet paper came as a surprise. The lack of it was not just due to a surge in demand but was said to be a result of hoarding. But why? As Justin Wolfers argued, showing that economists were unafraid to tell it like it is, "[o]nce they have more toilet paper, people aren't going to poo more."[9] He saw it like a bank run. People saw that toilet paper supplies were dwindling and bought more because they were concerned about supplies down the track. This created a run on the product just like a bank run. As it turned out, some toilet paper (even if it wasn't the good stuff) was back in the store after the initial rush before people found that they didn't have a square to spare.[10]

Hand sanitizer and other products that might be subject to real shortages are another matter. One story involved a couple of entrepreneurs who bought up a huge supply of hand sanitizer right after the first US death on March 1.[11] They had intended to sell their stock of 17,700 bottles at a large markup on Amazon. Before they could do so, Amazon cracked down, preventing them and others from selling the items that were in high demand. eBay followed suit. In the end, the bottles were donated to hospitals.

Price gouging is given an ugly name because, of course, it is associated with people taking advantage of shortages in times of crisis to make a profit. At normal times, economists usually like to let prices rise because they signal to others where demand is high and there are profitable opportunities to produce more. In other words, they are part of a market process for resource allocation. When we outlaw or otherwise try to provide a cap on prices, what we are doing is accepting a shortage.

As John Kenneth Galbraith, who headed up the US World War II office of price controls, noted, this is an acceptance of a "disequilibrium system" where demand persistently outstrips supply. This meant that items subject to controls needed to be rationed. As Galbraith noted, the outrage at this process tended to involve surprising items (just as we saw with toilet paper):

> [F]or some reason ceilings on fur coats inspired them to special anger. On several occasions I found myself contending with new colleagues (and once with a new administrator) who were enthusiastic about dropping price controls on fur coats. When

they saw that this action would put a premium on high-priced coat manufacture, would draw materials ("trim") away from cheaper lines, they soon reversed themselves. In doing so they adopted a position entirely consistent with a broad theoretical pattern for allocating resources and equalizing incentives. Of the existence of any such theoretical pattern they were totally unaware.[12]

Given this, it is instructive to consider why we happily resort to price controls in times of crisis. The reason is that it may well do a better job at resource allocation. According to research by Piotr Dworczak, Scott Kominers, and Mohammad Akbarpour,[13] whom we want to get hand sanitizer can be different from whom the market will allocate it to. In that case, the social value of who has sanitizer is unrelated to wealth. Thus, had the price gougers got their way, only the wealthy would have got their hands on it and, in the process, protected themselves and the people they interacted with from infection.[14] But those are the very people who have the best access to healthcare, who don't live in more densely populated neighborhoods, or who can easily work from home. What makes more social sense is for the poorer members of the community to be allocated the hand sanitizer. Price controls give them a fighting chance. What might even be better is directly allocating hand sanitizer supply according to where it can have the greatest impact.

Restrictions on Movement

We need to keep infected people isolated because one infected person can have the same impact as that of a mass shooter. Here is the calculation. If the R_0 for COVID-19 is 2, then an infected person will cause two others to be infected. But it obscures the magnitude of the problem. Those two people will infect two more people, and so on. After 10 rounds of this, that adds up to 1,024. (If $R_0 = 3$, it is 59,049!) If 1 percent of those people die from the disease, one infected person has been responsible for 10 deaths. Suffice it to say, that puts mass shootings in perspective. It is no surprise we want to keep infected people isolated.

The problem is how to do that. The first problem you face is the informational one. Coronavirus carriers are not marked with a hypothetical big red nose. For you to be isolated, you have to know if you are infected. With COVID-19, as was already explained in chapter 3, the majority of infected people may be unaware of it and exhibit no symptoms. A second problem is also informational: infected people might not want other people to know. This is something that will be explored more fully in chapter 8. People may fear being isolated because it might signal to others that they are dangerous. Or they may not wear a mask to signal to others their confidence in their own healthiness.

Absent information regarding whether individuals were infected, many governments opted for policies that restricted the movement of entire populations. If you had information, you would try to target both the individuals at risk from medical complications from the coronavirus and those people with a higher individual R_0. For COVID-19, some physicians and economists wondered if a more targeted approach could be achieved by restricting the movement of identifiable groups. For instance, as those over the age of 60 were more likely to require the higher end of health costs (including death) associated with the virus, would it be better to isolate them and leave the rest of the population to circulate?[15] Doing this would greatly mitigate the economic costs from a broader policy.[16]

The problem with targeting is that there are real doubts it would work. If a large proportion of those under 60 still become sick and need hospitalization, resources could still be overwhelmed. Moreover, with large numbers of infected younger people, we lack the people to support the elderly being isolated. As Alex Tabarrok argues, there are internal contradictions that may well render it impossible for a more "surgical" approach to social distancing.[17]

Targeted policies are also hard to enforce. When there are restrictions on movement, it is very easy for the authorities to see whether people are moving or not. In their absence it is harder to tell and can require more resources.[18] For these reasons, to deal with the costs associated with COVID-19 transmission, governments have opted for blanket policies akin to martial law in wartime or other times of emergency. These may be supported by penalties for violations but nothing like the type of taxes that economists would otherwise recommend so that exceptions can be made at the discretion of individual decision makers willing to bear a taxation cost. Instead, a heavy-handed approach is used without much room for nuance.

At the time of writing, social distancing has been proceeding for some months. In most countries, these policies were able to flatten the curve and reduce the numbers infected to low levels. In some countries, such as Australia and New Zealand, full suppression seemed possible. In others, the economic costs were weighing strongly and there was pressure to reopen economies. It is unknown whether these measures will continue to contain the spread of the virus or cause other outbreaks and additional rounds of lockdown.[19] We will discuss different strategies for reemergence from lockdowns in chapter 9.

Key Points

1. Pandemics require resolve and quick action to control while minimizing public health and the eventual economic impact. The urgency and need for coordination imply that governments need to adopt policies and allocate resources akin to times of war. This means a suspension of free market forces in favor of command and control approaches.

2. If social distancing aimed at "flattening the curve" is too late, the goal of that policy—to prevent healthcare systems from reaching capacity—will not be achieved. In that situation, governments will need to rapidly expand capacity using wartime protocols such as redirecting private manufacturing facilities to produce medical equipment and using the military to expand hospital capacity.

3. There is a need for price controls on products that have a role in reducing the spread of the infection, as market prices will not allocate those products where there are shortages in an optimal manner.

4. Restrictions on movement will need to be imposed and enforced to ensure proper social distancing in containing COVID-19. Targeted quarantines have high risks associated with them that may undermine their effectiveness unless information about those specifically infected is widely available.

6

This Time It Really Is Different

Recessions are not normally thought of as normal. But *normal* recessions tend to follow a certain pattern. First, they are preceded by a boom—a sustained period of high growth. Second, this boom gives the financial sector the confidence to innovate in various new ways of managing risk. Too often, however, these are not really new innovations per se but, instead—it is not a stretch to suggest—are just new ways of rationalizing the taking of risk and spreading it around. Third, some people start worrying about whether these new innovations are really innovations but are instead just more risk taking. Those worries are often dismissed by those in the mainstream who point out that, while that may have been the case in the past, *this time it really is different*, and the financial markets have found a party that will last forever. Fourth, something happens that starts to suggest this isn't a party anymore. Like Wile E. Coyote, the market realizes they are over a cliff and the party ends in a crash as if gravity is a force that can be defied without self-awareness. And, finally, this leads to a freeze in liquidity—that is, everyone not wanting to do anything but hold onto whatever money they have—which curtails investment, harms the cash flow of businesses, causes bankruptcies, and puts people out of work. The end result of this is an economic mess that the government and central banks try to solve by providing liquidity that went missing and by spending where others stopped, and, after a long period of time (at least for the unemployed), the economy starts up again and there is a boom. Repeat.

Given the regularity of the normal recession narrative, you may wonder how people could think there was something else going on. In hindsight, it all looks like a familiar pattern. At the time, however, there are people who think otherwise. They may class themselves as mavericks who will finally buck a historical trend, or it may be that they are a generation who didn't live through it before nor have taken or paid attention during their Macroeconomics 101 classes. But it is precisely because no one is really sure who believes what that during the actual cycle, there is uncertainty and noise. Indeed, financial markets have confidence issues all of the time and often manage to act like a recession is coming even when it does not emerge. That is, a financial crisis always precedes a recession, but there are financial crises that also happen without broader "real world" consequences. Such uncertainty is why governments and central banks can be (somewhat) excused when they don't quite see a recession coming and perhaps act when it is too late.

The COVID-19 pandemic is a real crisis and not a financial crisis born of years of naked hubris on the part of relatively few people. Instead, it has elements of a natural disaster and, surprisingly, as explained below, a national holiday. At the time of this writing, the COVID-19 recession is more of the latter than the former and the hope is to keep it that way. Either way, it is very different from previous recessions—we don't need hindsight to understand what its causes are. We know exactly what happened. Economic activity is falling because of COVID-19, both its (potential) impact and our policies designed to protect our health from it. From the perspective of economic policy, that yielded something unprecedented: virtually all economists—regardless of how confident or not they were in the economic role of the government—agreed on what we had to do about it.[1] We needed to ensure that people got paid or, at the very least, continued to act as if they were going to be paid.

Thus, with respect to the economic side of the equation, COVID-19 has turned the pandemic information problem on its head. We know what caused the recession and we know how to stop it. The information challenge is to ensure that everyone understands that and acts in that way—specifically, so that existing relationships are preserved and that when this is over the economy can just pick back up where it started from. But given that there is a real economic disruption, we have to work hard to make sure it doesn't end up leaving a wasteland of economic woe that requires long-term rebuilding to restore.

Before explaining the details of how to achieve this, it is useful to reflect on the natural disaster recession that, in many respects, we are trying to avoid. Such recessions have occurred in the past and they are the worst.

Dark Recessions

Economic activity is usually measured by exchange—that is, people pay money for services and things and one person's purchases becomes another's pay. The more we do this, the higher our incomes are. Recessions are a reduction in economic activity. As a consequence, we end up with lower incomes and lower expenditure. As expenditures tend to make us happier than not, our economic well-being is harmed by recessions.

There are two distinct ways that we can see a reduction in economic activity. First, we can decide that we want to spend less on things. If we do that, then businesses find their demand and sales will drop off; they will be less profitable and, not surprisingly, will want to scale back what they do. Fewer payments mean fewer people are paid. Second, something terrible can befall our ability to produce things that people will buy. If that happens, then, regardless of how much they may want those things, there will be shortages. If there are fewer people around to be paid, there will be fewer payments. Dark recessions are recessions of the second variety.

Natural disasters are a clear cause of dark recessions. A flood, hurricane, or earthquake can hit a region and, in the process, cost lives and destroy productive assets—in particular, buildings and equipment but also infrastructure. Ultimately, we produce things by supplying capital and labor. Natural disasters reduce the availability of both, and, depending on its severity, it can take months or years to restore them. If there is a silver lining here, we can ensure people get paid quickly by employing them in the cleanup and rebuilding process. From the perspective of our national accounts, disaster in reality doesn't always look like a disaster for the GDP.

The same loss in productive factors arises after wars. During wars there is another story as resources are reallocated to war efforts. Once again, this is a situation where a seeming expansion in economic activity underlies a tragedy.

A pandemic has the elements of a natural disaster except that it is purely focused on people. The fear is that a large share of the population will become sick and a relatively large share might die. From an economic perspective, that means that temporarily, and potentially permanently, we will have fewer workers to produce stuff. We will have a recession or worse but without the potential increase in economic activity that might be generated by rebuilding.

The past is some guide to this. The only global, widespread pandemic that has happened during times where we kept some economic data is the flu of 1918.[2] The problem, of course, is that the pandemic was hot off the heels of World War I, although it was precisely the end of that war and the returning soldiers that led to it being a global event. This made it hard to disentangle what was due to the war and what was due to the pandemic.

Economists Robert Barro, Jose Ursua, and Joanna Weng have looked at the impact of the 1918 influenza pandemic and have calculated that it likely resulted in the deaths of 2 percent of the world's population over a two-year period.[3] That put it in a class of disasters akin to the world wars and the Great Depression where there were greater than 10 percent declines in real per capita consumption in an adjacent year. Nonetheless, it is hard to separate the pandemic from the war.

To tease this out, the economists noted that World War I had different intensities of combat both on and away from a country's own soil and that there were some differences in how the pandemic spread across countries. They concluded that, in the United States, the pandemic fatality rate of 0.5 percent likely led to a decrease in GDP of 1.5 percent (2 percent for consumption) but that there was a corresponding decline through 1921 that caused a 6 percent decrease in GDP (7 percent for consumption) in that year alone. In other words, these were declines similar to the Great Recession of 2008–2009.

Could we be facing a dark recession that is worse than this? It is hard to say. On the "bright" side, unlike 1918, most of those becoming seriously ill are not of working age. On the "dark" side, we have more complex and integrated supply chains where an outbreak in a particular workplace or region can cause widespread disruptions. Even completely ignoring the horrific loss in life and uncertainty, a dark recession is very significant and something we want to work very hard to prevent.

The Recession We "Want"

A dark recession could come later. At the beginning of the outbreak, we have policies being enacted that are generating an immediate recession. This is the recession we want so as to prevent the catastrophic outcomes we really don't want. But that doesn't mean it isn't without costs.[4] In the United States alone, as of May 2020, the immediate unemployment numbers were at levels not seen since the Great Depression when 30 percent were out of work. It is, as former Obama economic advisor Austan Goolsbee said, a "now problem" that we want to "prevent forever damage."[5]

Small businesses are worried about both now and the future. The majority of countries are pursuing social distancing in response to the pandemic, which means that those businesses have found that, all of a sudden, their customers have disappeared and with them the payments they make. What hasn't disappeared are lots of bills. If you are a restaurant owner, you can scale back purchases of food and you could also lay off employees. In both cases, there is the specter of supply chain disruption, which is what many economic policy makers immediately worried about. But what those businesses cannot do is easily stop paying rent, loan repayments, utilities, and other costs that do not vary much (or at all) with customer volume.

Here is what normally happens if a business loses its customers. They scale back expenses, and then, if it continues, they are unable to pay for those other items and so go out of business. This is part of the ebb and flow of the economy and a reason for businesses to work hard to keep their customers coming. On the other side, there is little tolerance for unpaid bills because those suppliers—say, a landlord or a bank—have their own businesses to manage. This is why we measure economic activity by the volume of payments that are made between people in a year (as we do for GDP and its relatives). We are richer when we pay each other more and are poorer otherwise.

This time it really is different. We know exactly why businesses have seen their customers disappear—the pandemic response of social distancing, whether enforced or otherwise, wants to ensure that people do not congregate even if that is the way economic activity takes place. Moreover, we know that, ideally, we want people to go straight back to their economic activity afterward. In other words, in a normal recession we don't want to go back to business as usual because that likely caused the problem. In a pandemic, we do.

This may seem like a tough task, but we should take solace that we choose to have recessions all of the time and it just works out. This may seem like a surprising statement, but consider what happens on December 25 in many countries. On that day, economic activity declines at levels that would make the Great Depression seem like a picnic. Apart from some people who would really like Chinese food, this does not appear to have significant economic costs. You may want to work that day or you may want to buy something, but you will have difficulty finding others reciprocate in the transaction. Hence, payments stop and, with that, economic activity.

If we measured GDP changes daily rather than monthly or quarterly, this may show up in our economic mindset. The same is true of our "weekly recession" that occurs during what we call "the weekend." Once again, we appear to agree that no one is transacting as much on Saturdays or Sundays (or Fridays in some places), and even if you want to, you cannot engage in some forms of economic activity. It's a regular recession and one that we appear to want just to give everyone a break.

This is the reason why pandemic-induced social distancing that causes a recession is a little like a national holiday. We have agreed not to engage in economic activity, so we should not be surprised when our usual measures of such activity show a decline.

Herein lies our potential mistake: treating this recession like a normal recession when it is not. People are not getting paid and resources are lying idle. But that is what makes a recession and not the normal state of affairs. If we layer on the concern that the usual way of measuring economic activity is sending us bad signals, which is what happens in a normal recession, then we have a problem.[6]

It shouldn't be that way. Instead, we have to do what we do on weekends and holidays. We need to stop time.

The Pause

"Stopping time" is a lovely turn of phrase that I can attribute to Scott Ellison, who was quoted on the Marginal Revolution blog with this proposal:[7]

> I propose temporarily stopping time. This means that today's date, Tuesday, March 17th, 2020, will remain the current date until further notice. This also means that everything that happens in time (e.g. mortgage due dates, payrolls, travel bookings, stock market trading, contractor gigs, concerts, sporting events) will be paused. It also means that all of these events remain on the books, and will continue as planned once time is resumed.

He notes that most do this every fall when we all agree that time will be paused one hour and pretend that we deserved more sleep. The problem, however, is that much of the economy needs to actually keep running—some more intensively than before—which means that just calling a time-out won't do the trick.

The principle, though, is a useful one. Without something different, a business that finds itself in trouble will have to shut down. Shutdowns are costly precisely because it is hard to get started again. Our hypothetical restaurant owner would have to find a new place, secure new capital, and make new investments, all before hiring people and opening up. It is like hitting the eject button and removing the CD from the player. Instead (and you can anticipate a tortured metaphor here), what the restaurant owner wants to do is hit the pause button. They want their business to stay where it is but to stop playing.[8]

One obvious solution is for the private sector to be able to do this for themselves. Sure, our restaurant owner's landlord could evict them because they are no longer able to pay rent. But the landlord could also not do that. They could realize—because it is plainly obvious—that the restaurant is a viable business in the middle of a hiccup and so agree to suspend rent payments. In actuality, they may not be technically losing out from this choice because (1) they are unlikely to find any other renter in the meantime and (2) they won't have to look for another renter beyond that.

This is all well and good if the landlord has the power to make such decisions. However, behind many landlords are banks that have provided them with mortgages. They have provided loans to many property owners and may struggle to work out who is really participating in the pause. Thus, they may choose to foreclose on the landlords. If we could all see what was going on, maybe we could coordinate the pause without help. However, because that is risky and the pause button needs to be hit urgently, governments can help coordinate that just as they do with daylight savings time.

This is not specific to rent or mortgage payments by small businesses. The services that comprise their fixed costs extend well beyond that. The popular fresh fast food chain in Boston, Clover Food Lab, put out a plea in March 2020 for tech companies to not require payments for three months.[9] Its founder, Ayr Muir, wrote:

> I'm hours and hours into painstakingly reaching out to the HUGE number of services Clover uses to operate. For all it's the same thing. (1) We want to use these services as soon as we re-open, (2) we DON'T want to lose all our data and set-up all over again, (3) We CAN'T pay while we have no revenues coming in.

Some companies responded to Muir's plea, but the majority did not. For companies that have otherwise very high margins, a pause would be a sensible response compared with pushing businesses off their services and making them pay the costs—in time and otherwise—of setting up again. The difference between these Big Tech companies and landlords is that it is highly likely they won't face any costs from offering a pause.

All of these considerations apply beyond small business. There are employees who face consequences in terms of paying ongoing household expenses should they find themselves unemployed. So, while we cannot necessarily expect them to be paid while not working for an extended period of time, the pause notion surely equally applies to them with respect to their rent, mortgage, debt, and utility payments.[10]

How to Pause

For once, it didn't take governments long to realize the nature of the problem. Through March 2020 they ordered lenders and landlords to hit the pause button on foreclosures and evictions for a month or two.[11] French President Emmanuel Macron was more strident and suspended utility payments and rent for small businesses, promising that "no business would be allowed to fail."[12] The US government pushed back its annual tax payment deadline from April 15 to July 15 and allowed student loan payments to be stopped without penalty. But perhaps no country opted to "freeze" their economy quicker than Denmark. In mid-March 2020, they opted to pay 75 percent of all salaries of potentially laid off workers (earning up to $52,000 a year), guarantee 70 percent of new bank loans to companies, and cover the fixed expenses of small businesses. The total cost was 13 percent of their usual GDP.[13] If the United States did the same thing, it would be $2.5 trillion.

Halting consequences and payments is a very direct way of pausing the economy and making sure that the temporary harm is not baked into the recovery. In other cases, the government tried to provide money to achieve the same thing. In Canada and the United Kingdom this included wage subsidies when businesses keep employees and delayed tax payments that businesses make on their behalf.

Perhaps the most radical proposal came from French economists Emmanuel Saez and Gabriel Zucman, who argued that governments should become "payers of the last resort."[14] If a business was facing shutdown, the government would come in and pay for employees and for fixed-cost payments such as rent, utilities, and interest. In other words, they would have governments pay for businesses to pause. They suggested that unemployment payments could simply be made as if workers have lost their jobs, to provide an easy route to such payments. They would also allow self-employed or gig economy workers to report themselves as idle to be eligible for such payments. For businesses, if they are part of lockdowns for more extreme social distancing, they would report their costs, be reimbursed, and then any misreporting would be worked out later.

Is it better to stop bill payments or to pay them? Stopping certain bill payments is straightforward and easy to enforce. The problem, of course, is that it is not clear we are allocating the burden of preventing a recession equitably. In fact, when the dust settles, that won't be the case. The problem is that, at the moment the policy needs to be introduced, there is no easy way of knowing this. This suggests that there may be some political fallout or economic recompense to be hashed out post-crisis. That uncertainty may actually cause some short-term problems to become long-term ones.

By contrast, paying bills can circumvent this by, in principle, sharing the burden at the outset. For instance, you could make sure that the hit to workers in terms of lost income was proportionate to the likely loss in capital returns. This is done by paying part of the invoiced amount of bills and wages. The challenge with this is that it requires some verification (eventually) of what those bills might have been and, in the meantime, a process of getting those payments to where they are needed. In other words, neither of these options is cleanup free.[15]

An Alternative: Income-Contingent Loans

The problem with both stopping bill payments or paying them is that each becomes more difficult the longer the initial pandemic recession lasts. What is more, we do not actually have a good sense of how much more difficult these would become. In other words, they are really temporary emergency measures.

One measure that has the potential to last longer is government or private loans with a government guarantee. At the time of writing, various government support loans are being contemplated. As Sendhil Mullainathan wrote:

> During the 2008 crisis, the government understood this principle well. It bailed out large financial firms for much the same reason: They were facing temporary shocks that, without intervention, would unnecessarily become permanent ones. Whatever else one may feel about those bailouts, that economic logic was sound. Those investments yielded healthy profits for the government.[16]

The same logic of using loans has also been considered for some of the more hard-hit industries, including travel and hospitality. Loans are a way of allowing bills to be paid without having to sort out what bills and how much because whoever takes out a loan is still responsible for repayments.

However, it may also be the case, given the absence of revenue or wages, that full loans may be not be financially possible. In this regard, there is a debate regarding whether governments should step in and handle some of the short-term payments to give debtors financial breathing space or to provide support to reduce the loan principal. The rationale for the latter is that it reduces the future debt overhang of businesses and others, assisting them in getting back on their feet.

A careful study by Peter Ganong and Pascal Noel showed that if your goal is to prevent temporary issues from becoming long-term ones, it is better to provide short-term help.[17] Using the differential impact of certain programs offered during the financial crisis of 2008–2009, they were able to measure the impact of reducing long-term obligations (a direct improvement to wealth) versus reducing short-term payments (assisting liquidity). As it turned out, the former did nothing for borrowers who were already underwater, while the latter significantly reduced default rates. This study strongly suggests that we want to help borrowers with government-backed assistance for loan repayments rather than assistance paid directly to lenders to reduce loan principals.

Of course, providing this assistance to people directly can make it hard to tailor it to individual circumstances as well as to ensure that the repayment of any assistance is not onerous. As it turns out, however, an innovative Australian debt scheme used for higher education tuition could be readily applied. Australian universities are (mostly) public but still charge tuition to students. The rationale for that is that while education has public benefits, when you have an education you are the main financial beneficiary and so should be responsible for some of the costs. Thus, in the 1990s, the left-wing Labor government ended two decades of free tuition and put in its place an income-contingent loan.

The idea was this. You want to ensure that student loans are automatic and not onerous to administer. Thus, when tuition was charged, students could opt not to pay it immediately but, instead, to incur a debt to the government. However, what you did not want is the repayment of those loans to depend too much on career paths. After all, a lawyer or doctor may be able to earn more than a high school teacher, so you don't want the latter to have debt repayments that presumed too high an income. The scheme instead gave students a slightly higher marginal tax rate until their loan principal (plus modest interest) was repaid. Thus, the high-income professionals would, by virtue of their higher income, be required to pay more sooner than those with lower income.

Higher education was a natural candidate for this type of loan, but in 2004, my economist colleague Stephen King and I proposed a similar arrangement for housing.[18] We suggested that when there were temporary shocks to someone's income as might arise should they lose employment, then rather than evicting or foreclosing on them (as would be their initial worry), the government would step in and cover those housing-related payments for a time. A debt would accrue, but, as for students, it would only be repaid through the tax system, when people had income again. This would both provide stability for households when there were economic shocks and also, by providing financial breathing space, make lending or offering housing to people who might be more exposed to such shocks a better proposition for lenders and landlords.

There is little reason that such a scheme could not be enacted to cover short-term expenses associated with a pandemic recession. Presumably, only those who believed that they could pause their economic activity would avail themselves of this loan, but then they could spread the burden over time. It would provide liquidity but at the same time ensure that those who received payments were responsible for them somewhat in proportion to their benefits.[19]

The Final Stimulus

In many respects, the previous discussion is a somewhat optimistic one. It assumes governments can implement policies that pause the economy and that actually work. Since it has never been done before, economists have no idea whether it will be enough. Conceptually, it is a strong proposal. In reality, as with all of these things, there are consequences we cannot predict.

There is a pessimistic scenario. Rather than bounce back after the pandemic has abated, the effects on economic activity may be long-lasting.[20] During the crisis, households may have seen their savings been drawn down and, having experienced an economic disaster, may be reluctant to spend without restoring those savings. That, in turn, will make it hard for businesses to rebuild and rehire, which will make people even more reluctant to turn back on their new-found thriftiness. The end result may be a recession that lasts many years. To forestall this outcome, governments may need to aggressively stimulate the post-crisis economy.

Bound up in the US approach to macroeconomic support in the United States is a program to send a stimulus check of $1,200 to every citizen as restrictions were put in place. This was also done after 9/11 and during the 2008 financial crisis, in the form of tax rebates. The idea then, as now, is to restore consumer confidence and spending. With COVID-19 or any pandemic, as the recession is not normal, one must wonder if such direct stimulus is appropriate. The worry is that, while this cash may support those people who have loan and other immediate obligations, with social distancing policies in place, the money may not be consumed but instead saved. Saving can be beneficial if there is a need for liquidity, but in this case, that was already being provided by aggressive actions from central banks.

The determination of when a direct stimulus is likely to be required is part of the effort to restart the economy as physical interactions return to normal. Thus, we might be concerned that directing policy toward a stimulus prematurely might hamper that option arising later and might detract from the decidedly not-normal task of pausing the economy at the outset of the crisis.

Key Points

1. The worst economic outcome from COVID-19 is a dark recession where there are insufficient workers available to restore economic activity to its previous level.

2. To prevent this, we had to engineer a recession that would accompany social distancing to contain the outbreak. In doing this, the key objective was to be able to preserve job matches and prevent businesses from closing so that economic activity can be restarted again.

3. This required payments, subsidies, and loan guarantees that can ensure that people's short-term disruptions are not translated into long-term breakups that would require a lengthy period of time to overcome. One way of doing this would be to institutionalize loans by the government that could be paid back through taxes when incomes (or business revenue) is restored.

4. Following the crisis, there will likely be a need for the usual macroeconomic policies to stimulate and accelerate the recovery.

7

The Testing Economy

The cows were not safe. They were mad. But what made them unsafe was that anyone consuming them may well become mad. That is what the United Kingdom discovered in the 1990s. It was found that cattle affected by bovine spongiform encephalopathy (BSE) could cause a variant of Creutzfeldt–Jakob disease in humans. That disease would mentally impair its victims and eventually take their lives. As of 2013, 177 people in the United Kingdom had died. Not surprisingly, no one wanted to consume cattle that might have BSE.

The reaction of the United States to cases of BSE is instructive. In 2003, a cow imported to the United States from Canada was found to have BSE. Imports were banned. In Canada, cattle prices fell by a half and retail beef prices by 14 percent. Canada's annual beef export revenues to the United States fell by two thirds. At the time, Canadian beef made up three quarters of US beef imports, so this imposed costs on both countries, with losses estimated in the billions.[1] When, later in 2003, an infected cow was discovered in Washington State, the trade bans fell on the other foot.

As internal bans were neither palatable nor practical, the US Department of Agriculture (USDA) ramped up testing. It favored what was argued to be a less accurate "rapid" immunologic test (with results delivered in hours rather than weeks). The cost of these tests was about $200 million, but the positive impact on reviving the US beef export industry was far in excess of this.

This chapter is about the value of testing and how it can improve the functioning of markets when there are infectious diseases. The BSE example indicates the value of testing for the beef trade and has strong lessons in the wake of COVID-19 for how the testing of humans can make it safe for people to interact with one another. But before getting to the meat (!) of the issue, there was one more twist in the USDA's handling of BSE testing. Having successfully demonstrated the economic value of tests, the USDA promptly banned them.

You read that right. The USDA forbade cattle exporters from paying for the tests themselves for their own livestock. A producer of black Angus beef for sale to Japan, Creekstone Farms Premium Beef, wanted to use the USDA's approved rapid test as part of its production and marketing efforts. The reasons were obvious. It was commercially lucrative to provide that information to customers. However, the USDA claimed that using the test was for "surveillance" purposes and was concerned that if some producers tested their cattle, this would imply that the cattle of others was unsafe. Cattle trade associations feared that this would lead to an unraveling, necessitating all producers to incur the costs of testing.

Creekstone sued the USDA and, initially, prevailed.[2] The USDA's position wasn't ludicrous as a matter of economics. Many economists had been concerned that in some markets, particularly higher education, there may be undue costs to signaling and that there may be a social rationale for banning such contests.[3] (For instance, students spending enormous effort to get into a slightly higher-ranked college even though the learning outcomes were the same.) However, in this situation, the Court realized that there was a customer who was particularly sensitive about certification of quality and that in the absence of a threat to public safety, there was no reason to prevent a business's right to use tests to assist in their marketing. The only rationale for prohibiting the use of the test would be if the tests were uninformative. They weren't. In other words, the tests could not simultaneously be effective in identifying a safety concern and ineffective in certifying product quality. The USDA appealed and the US Court of Appeals reversed the decision and returned to the USDA the power to regulate BSE test kits, which it exercised. Private testing was banned.

Testing = Information

The interests of economy and public health collide because the most important way to deal with a pandemic in the interests of public health is to slow the rate of infection (that is, R_0). A person having a disease is a health problem that requires knowing how to treat that person and then doing so. A person having an *infectious* disease is a public health problem because, in addition, that person can pass the disease onto others. Being infectious is what turns an isolated health problem into an interdependent one. Because our typical dealings with other people rely on others being safe to interact with, pandemics destroy interactions and, consequently, the economy.

The BSE infections showed a microcosm of how a lack of safety impacts interactions—in this case, between cattle and humans. But they also showed the importance of knowledge, which is the theme of this book.

The key to making people safe is knowledge. One way that can occur is to let the virus run its course without interventions. Of course, that is tantamount to saying that public health will not be prioritized over the economy. In the United States, that likely would have meant 15 million hospitalized at the peak and more sick at home. And up to 3 million might have died. That is the underpinning of the dark recession scenario. Suffice it to say, if the goal is to make people safe for interactions, making them completely unsafe for a period of time would appear to defeat the point.

Make People Safe Again

How do we gather that knowledge? The answer with respect to COVID-19 is tests.[4] There are two types of tests that are relevant. First, there are tests that can indicate the presence of the coronavirus in an individual. Second, there are tests that can indicate the presence of COVID-19 antibodies. One type—commonly known as a PCR test—tests whether you have the virus and are likely to be infectious (e.g., equivalent to the Rudolph thought experiment in chapter 1), while the other—serological—tests whether you have had the virus and are likely to be immune. At the onset of the COVID-19 outbreak, tests for the presence of the virus were available, and, depending on the country and the test, there were differences in how quickly they could yield a result. As of the time of writing, antibody tests are being developed but are not verified, let alone widely available.[5] The two types of tests, which I will refer to as HAVE and HAD, respectively, play different roles in making people safe.[6]

The first thing to note is that a HAVE testing regime potentially makes a HAD test redundant. With a perfect HAVE testing regime, you would test everyone at a regular interval and the test would, with high confidence, tell you if you have the virus or not. Given this, on the assumption that having the virus would give you immunity, you would not expect to learn much more from a HAD test.

For COVID-19, no country has a perfect HAVE testing regime. In general, as tests are not widely available, different jurisdictions have different policies regarding the factors that, if present, might require a test. This is somewhat paradoxical because, if you had COVID-19 symptoms (such as a fever, cough, or shortness of breath), you were more likely to test positive for the virus. Thus, if a person with symptoms had a positive test, this is actually *less* information than would be gained if a person without symptoms had a positive test result. Put simply, the more observable are your COVID-19 symptoms, the less valuable a test is.

This is especially the case as many infected people are, in fact, asymptomatic. At the time of writing, the extent to which asymptomatic people are infectious is unclear. However, what is understood is that some symptoms, particularly a cough, can make people more infectious.

Moreover, one value of testing is that it can inform public health officials of the characteristics of the disease, including the base epidemiological properties such as R_0 and how infectious asymptomatic carriers were. If you test symptomatic people and find that, say, 80 percent of them have COVID-19, then without knowing how many asymptomatic people have the virus, you only know that a random person in the population likely has COVID-19 with less than 80 percent probability and not how much less.

Fortunately, there were situations where HAVE testing was conducted without reference to underlying symptoms. One case was the Diamond Princess cruise ship that was quarantined in Japan for a period of time and ended up having many victims. However, a cruise ship does not match the properties in the population in terms of like transmission rates (it is a unique situation) nor in terms of other factors such as mortality (as the demographics were different). A better indication came from a proactive study of the town of Vò in Italy, whose entire population of 3,300 was tested and retested regardless of symptoms. It was discovered there that half of the positive cases were asymptomatic.[7]

The Vò experience also highlighted the effectiveness of using HAVE tests to identify who should be isolated. The first testing round found 3 percent of the population with the virus. They were isolated, and a second round of test found only 0.3 percent still infected. Importantly, that was not zero and there were still six infected people who also had no symptoms. Identifying them prevented a reemergence of the infection in the population.

There is one final remark to make regarding testing and symptoms. Symptoms are themselves a type of test albeit one with error. For instance, one cost-effective way of regular testing is taking temperatures. These are done at some border crossings and other places where there might be large gatherings of people. The problem with this test is that an elevated temperature may be consistent with other things—for example, the flu. This can be important, as shown in table 5.1.

Notice that, alongside fever, other symptoms are common to both COVID-19 and the flu. The main symptoms that are more clearly common with COVID-19 than the flu are shortness of breath and respiratory issues. Thus, it is these symptoms that give the clearest indication that a person has COVID-19.[8] They may, of course, be hard to measure if they are mild, as the baseline may differ between individuals.[9]

There is one method that would assist in targeting asymptomatic people for testing and then isolation: *contact tracing*.[10] This requires

Table 5.1

Symptom	COVID-19	Flu
Fever	Common	Common
Cough	Common	Common
Fatigue	Common	Common
Runny nose	Sometimes	Sometimes
Headache	Sometimes	Common
Body aches	Sometimes	Common
Shortness of breath	Common	Sometimes
Respiratory issues	Common	Sometimes

Source: Adapted from https://www.medicalnewstoday.com/articles/corona virus-vs-flu#symptoms.

an intensive effort to identify those persons who came in contact with someone who tested positive for COVID-19 (or was otherwise suspected to carry it) over the past week or so. In doing this, those people can be identified and then prioritized for tests (and potentially further contact tracing) even if they do not exhibit symptoms. This is especially useful if the virus is spread by so-called superspreaders (infected people who have contact with many people in a short period of time).[11] Again, the goal with testing or gathering information is to be able to isolate people on a more targeted basis than blanket policies that lock down entire regions.[12]

To summarize, a HAVE test is useful because it enables an action. That action is to isolate or quarantine any individual with a positive test until such time as they are held (through additional testing or otherwise) to no longer be infectious. The value of this strategy is that it is potentially more cost-effective (in terms of impact on economic and social life) than using blanket isolation policies to reduce rates of infection.[13] In this way, the availability and use of HAVE testing is a potential way in which countries can reduce the extent of the decrease in production possibilities during a pandemic.[14]

Watch for Rebounds

Testing is a straightforward way to solve the pandemic information gap. By knowing who is infected and taking them out of the population, you can reduce the rate at which the virus circulates. But economists are known as "dismal" scientists for a reason. What if doing testing changes the human equation?

Casting doubt on policies that "normal" people consider obviously sensible has a long tradition in economics. Back in the 1960s, safety advocates called for laws to make seat belts compulsory in all cars. This makes sense. If you wear a seatbelt you save lives. Enter economist Sam Peltzman. Peltzman noted that when you are wearing a seatbelt, you are, indeed, safer.[15] But that also means that, as a driver, you don't have to work as hard to drive safely. So even if drivers and their passengers are safer, there may be more accidents. He showed this led to harm elsewhere—most notably pedestrians.[16]

Could the same thing happen if people feel safer in pandemics due to testing? We do not really know yet. But as a matter of theory, it is certainly possible. Testing reduces the risk of encountering an infected person in your daily activities. Thus, if before testing, you were afraid of such encounters, the better the testing is, the less afraid you are. This means that some people will be less willing to practice social distancing (and other good behaviors such as mask-wearing). Now if everyone were tested, this wouldn't be an issue, as that decrease in social distancing would be safe and, indeed, the whole point in overcoming the pandemic information gap. But it is unlikely everyone will be tested. Instead, with only a fraction of the population tested, then, as people socially distance less, there will be more infections from that. Will the overall rate of infection rise? It depends on whether the testing removes infected people at a larger rate than reduced social distancing increases infections. The point is that it is not certain that a rebound effect, like the one observed in automobile safety, could occur.[17]

There are ways to mitigate this possibility. One way would be to identify the groups of people that are most likely to reduce their social distancing and ramp up testing for them. Another would be to combine testing with continual mandatory social distancing to ensure that rebounds can't take place. Either way, when you factor in the human equation, you have to be somewhat cautious when thinking testing will be an instant cure-all for an already significant pandemic.

Certified Safe

While the initial response to the COVID-19 pandemic in many countries (especially in Europe and North America) has been varying degrees of blanket isolation, there will come a time when those isolation policies need to be relaxed. Because HAVE testing has been either nonexistent for most or otherwise imperfect, the only safe individuals to be removed from isolation have been those who were known to have COVID-19 and recovered. Because COVID-19 can be asymptomatic, even if a large share of the population did have the virus at one point, even they may not be sure they are now immune. More broadly, even if they suspect they are immune, there would no easy way to communicate to others that they were safe.

Perhaps no example better illustrates the desire for certification of immunity than what happened during the yellow fever plague that hit New Orleans in the 1800s. In 1853 alone, one in 10 died. The only known defense was "acclimation"—to contract the disease and not die from it. You had a 50-50 chance of that last step. Historian Kathryn Olivarius documented that, despite this, the city (and its region) managed to grow. She recounts the experience of a German immigrant Vincent Nolte:

> Nolte cherished one form of capital above all. In 1806, three months after his arrival in New Orleans, he was bitten by a tiny mosquito and fell sick with yellow fever, the most terrifying disease in the Atlantic World. . . . Nolte survived his "acclimation." And now what had made him sick made him strong. He possessed "immunocapital": socially acknowledged lifelong immunity to a highly lethal virus, providing access to previously inaccessible realms of economic, political, and social power.[18]

In New Orleans an acclimation certificate was a key asset that determined whether you could engage in economic activity. Indeed, it was so valuable that many immigrants arriving actively tried to get sick, as this would be a ticket to economic prosperity and marriage if they survived.[19] Unfortunately, without a test, it turned out that the best way to become certified was to prove that you lived in a yellow fever–affected area for more than two years.

Contrary to the options available in the nineteenth century, in order to make the labor market safe again at some point, most countries will likely need to deploy HAD tests widely. Those who are found to have the requisite antibodies can then be certified safe. Obviously, this will require careful recording and verification of HAVE test results as well. Then some method of identifying the safe individuals will need to be devised. All this is within the realm of our current institutions and technology, but setting up the apparatus will likely be costly and require some time.[20] Indeed, one could imagine innovative ways of rationing access to such tests when they are scarce—say, by testing in conjunction with blood donations, thereby encouraging that activity as people try to establish their immunocapital.

While the notion of identifying immune and not immune people makes sense in terms of management of the pandemic, it is important to note that, as the New Orleans experience shows, there are potential risks. First, having immunity confers benefits on individuals that may cause those who have not had COVID-19 to try to become infected—especially if they are in a lower risk category for serious health issues. The problem here is that that could increase the risk of infections spreading quickly via those people or, as everyone is rolling the dice, a spike in demand for hospital services. These issues may be countered by phasing in HAD tests and certification.[21]

Second, HAD tests may not be perfect, which poses an issue for how they are relied on. To see this, suppose that the best HAD test involved a 5 percent chance of making a mistake (i.e., a false positive or negative). Suppose that in a population of 100 million, 10 percent were likely previously infected and immune. In this case, if you ran that HAD test, you would find 14 million who were immune. This is higher than those who are actually immune because you falsely certify 4.5 million of the nonimmune 90 million as immune and you also miss 500,000 of the immune. Thus, some carrying an immune certification would have just less than a 66 percent chance of being immune. This problem arises because the test has too many false positives (certifying people inaccurately) and the number of those immune in the population is relatively low.[22] The accuracy of the certification could be bolstered by information based on HAD tests and COVID-19 diagnoses, but, in reality, HAD tests will be able to provide reliable information on individuals (even if they are more accurate) only when the virus has spread through a larger share of the population.[23]

Finally, the question that will arise is what to do with people who do not test positive for HAVE or HAD. One option is for them to remain isolated, but the difficulty here is that there is no obvious end date for that policy. Another policy would be to have guidelines and other preventative measures imposed on those people that limit their interactions with other people who have negative HAVE tests, because if one of those people does end up contracting the disease, they would be able to transmit it to other people who have not yet had it. Overall, the right policy will depend on the proportion of people who test negative. If few people test negative, those negative-testing people are safer as they return to normal economic life because their chances of interacting with other nonimmune people are reduced. Moreover, the tests can assist in certifying people for interactions with high risk to others such as older people or in high-contact fields such as healthcare.

Nonetheless, the downside and potentially unavoidable consequence of moving to a testing economy in this way is that it will reduce social cohesion. Just as the beef producers who worried that having some producers become certified as BSE safe would cause producers who were not certified to be seen as unsafe, we should be concerned that not being certified safe might become stigmatized with all of the costs that entails.

How Safe Is Safe Enough?

The discussion here thus far has glossed over an important issue with any kind of test: that it is imperfect. In particular, a test conducted on a person who has COVID-19 can return negative—this is a false negative—while a test conducted on a person who doesn't have the virus can be returned positive—a false positive. This impacts on policies that are contingent on test results.

Recall that with a HAVE test, what we want to do is isolate those who test positive and release those who test negative. We are doing this to prevent having to isolate everyone. Thus, if a person has a false positive, relative to the fact that our plan was to isolate that person anyhow, the fact that we choose to isolate them impacts them but not by much relative to the alternative. By contrast, if a person has a false negative, our plan is to release that person from isolation. In that case, however, we are putting someone we wanted to isolate into the population. Suffice it to say, that is costly.

But is it so costly that we should not use a "test, then release" strategy? Typically, there is a trade-off between false positive and false negative rates, with one rising while the other falls. Often this is because a test is a test not just for one factor but for the presence of multiple factors. So, if your test involves looking for the presence of, say, three factors, then you might choose to conclude that the test is positive only if all three factors are present.[24] That means that, given this approach, you are less likely to have a false positive test but more likely to have a false negative test. This along with improperly done nose swabs is why for many COVID-19 tests there was a reported false negative rate of between 10 and 15 percent (in line with other viruses) but a false positive rate of only 1 percent.[25]

One reason many tests appear to err on the side of minimizing false positives is because antiviral treatments might be harmful to some patients or otherwise involve costs, and you do not want to use them on people who do not have a particular virus. By contrast, a false negative test can be followed up with a future test for that patient that may reverse the finding. In other words, you want to be confident that you are treating the right person, and if you have the option to continue observation and test, you may then be comfortable perhaps initially missing a treatable person.

This weight of characteristics changes when you are dealing with a different decision—whether to release a potentially infectious person. In that case, you would want to err on the side of minimizing false negatives. If you want to release someone who has tested negative, you may not have an option to retest them before they do more harm. By contrast, if someone tests positive falsely, you can keep them isolated and then retest them later. This same logic applies to both HAVE and HAD tests but is stronger for HAD tests as the goal is not to retest using that regime. By contrast, a HAVE regime would involve repeated testing of people who returned negative results in the past.

This suggests that our medical practices will need to be informed by the decisions that have to be made—treatment versus release—to an extent that we haven't done to this date. Of course, it goes without saying that tests that can reduce both false positives and false negatives will be more valuable as well. Interestingly, however, our tolerance for tests with errors may be greater than would be apparent at first. For instance, Nobel laureate economist Paul Romer conducted simulations of the movement of infectious diseases like COVID-19 through the population and compared the use of a blanket isolation strategy versus a test and release strategy even when tests had high degrees of false negatives.[26] His analysis suggested that even tests with a false negative rate of 20 percent or more could lead to two or three times fewer people eventually infected than a no-isolation approach but also involves fewer people required to be in isolation when even imperfect tests are used.

> It is not hard to see why targeting the isolation based on test results reduces the total number of people in isolation. What matters for controlling the infection is how many infectious people it isolates. If people are isolated at random, you have to isolate a lot more to get the same number of people who are infectious.[27]

The good news here is that, while we may want to calibrate test efficacy for the decision made, there is substantial room for error to still have a substantive impact. In other words, a more perfect test is better but not that much better than an imperfect one.[28] Nonetheless, even with very intense testing (say, everyone being tested once every two weeks), this will likely only reduce the intensity of required social distancing and contact tracing. That said, as those activities are the costliest for the economy, it is likely that the social rate of return to widespread testing will be very high. More practically, it is likely that the best option would be to be sensible in how tests are allocated and conducted.[29] For instance, in situations where households have been locked down for a month or more, perhaps only one member of a household needs to be tested.

Seeing the Big Picture

While widespread testing of the population is the key to solving the pandemic information problem, it is important to note that testing is also critically important just to see the big picture of how the virus is affecting the population and to forecast what needs to be done to reduce the spread of the virus. That is, testing is a way of obtaining critical population-level information on just how many people are likely to have already had COVID-19 and may be immune. It can inform government policy actions just as it can potentially inform individual responses.[30]

The need for testing for the purposes of surveillance rather than individual isolation decisions arises with respect to the uncertainty with regard to the fatality rate for COVID-19. In a situation where you cannot identify infected people, you can see the overall effect by looking at the number of COVID-19 fatalities. The problem here is that, in many countries, these were recorded only if the death was linked directly to a patient diagnosed (perhaps with a test) as having the novel coronavirus. But as the crisis continued, health officials realized that they may be missing some cases. In the United States, for example, there was a spike in deaths in poorer communities where people had been discovered in their homes without having visited a hospital. This was attributed to the lack of universal healthcare that made people reluctant to visit emergency rooms. Similarly, in other countries, deaths in aged-care facilities were not initially included as COVID-19 fatalities. However, when excess deaths over previous baselines were recorded, the impact of the pandemic was apparent. Overall, because only symptomatic people are tested, the recorded fatality rate is much higher than the true fatality rate.

This matters because if the true fatality rate is high, then that means that far fewer people have been infected and are potentially immune. Put simply, if the majority of people who contract the disease die from it, low numbers of deaths suggest low numbers of infections and, in turn, low numbers of survivors with immunity. In such a case, easing a lockdown may well lead to another outbreak. If the true fatality rate is low, then this is good news on two fronts. First, the disease is less of a concern for health. Second, the deaths observed are indications of many more infections and so it is safer to lift any lockdown as more people are likely to be immune. For this reason, conducting a wide, randomized study with an accurate HAVE test could reveal what the true fatality rate is and inform health policy.[31]

What If It's Worse?

Everything in this book thus far, as well as policy discussions regarding COVID-19, has been based on a very important assumption: once you have contracted the virus and recovered, you are immune. It is for this reason that epidemiologists focus on a sufficient share of the population obtaining immunity from COVID-19 either by past infection or as a result of a future vaccine. If you do this, then even with normal physical interactions, the virus eventually dies out (as R_0 becomes less than 1). In particular, this is why we can talk about HAVE and HAD testing as making people safe again. So, while the crisis is awful, the promise of immunity gives us hope.

What if that hope is unfounded? What if you are not immune even if you have contracted the virus? What if a vaccine is not possible for the same reason? In this case, epidemiologists no longer use the SIR (susceptible–infected–removed) model, as there are no recovered people who are not able to infect others. Instead, we must use the SIS (susceptible–infected–susceptible) model. In that situation, when R_0 exceeds one, the virus never goes away and a share of the population is always infected.[32] The only way to get rid of the virus is by extreme measures—for instance, socially distancing until there are no more infected people or by coming up with treatments such that we don't care if people are infected or not.[33]

Is this outcome possible for COVID-19? Because the virus is relatively new, at the time of writing, it is hard to be sure.[34] Because recovering from COVID-19 required antibodies, scientists were optimistic that such antibodies would give immunity for some period of time. However, in April 2020, South Korea reported 111 coronavirus patients testing positive again after they had recovered (and tested negative twice in a twenty-four-hour period).[35] One possibility is that the negative tests were false negatives. Another is that the virus has reactivated. This occurs when a virus is latent for a time and but remains inside the cells of the host. This happens with chickenpox, which can decades later reactivate in adults as shingles. Finally, there could be reinfection. This is why the flu is persistent. The antibodies provide immunity only for a time and not against alternative strains of the virus. Coronaviruses are a relatively recent phenomenon, so a lack of immunity remains a possibility.

Let's take that worst-case scenario and presume that infected patients are not permanently immune. One implication is that HAD tests are of little value. Similarly, a vaccine will not be our savior. Nonetheless, HAVE testing could be of value. While the intensity of testing would have to be even higher than what might otherwise be envisaged, the procedure of isolating those who test positive will reduce the ability of infected people to spread the virus around. In this situation, so long as this results in the rate at which those are being infected falling below the rate at which people are recovering from an instance of the infection, the pandemic can be contained, and the virus will eventually be wiped out.

This highlights another reason to invest in the testing economy. When it comes to HAVE tests, these are valuable whether the virus leads to immunity or not, or something in between. As a policy, they are a hedge against this uncertainty.

A Tale of Two Regions

Some countries moved to a testing economy very early in the COVID-19 pandemic. For instance, Taiwan started testing travelers from Wuhan for symptoms on December 31, 2019, and soon after integrated travel histories with national data sets and made them available to hospitals.[36] But Taiwan has special characteristics that make its response somewhat atypical (e.g., Taiwan is an island with a tight relationship with China). More instructive in terms of seeing what a testing economy can achieve is to compare the Lombardy and Veneto regions of Italy.

Both regions applied social distancing and locked down retail areas. But only Veneto put in place a testing regime: testing both symptomatic and asymptomatic cases, testing contacts if some-one tested positive, having testing carried out in homes, and implementing general measures to protect healthcare profession-als.[37] The result was that, as of March 26, Veneto (with a population of 5 million) had 7,000 cases and 287 deaths, while Lombardy (with a population of 10 million) had five times the number of cases and 5,000 deaths.

The testing economy is what emerges when you have the virus under control, but you do not have widespread immunity either via past infections or from a vaccine. This means that tests, like post-9/11 security measures, will likely be a part of our daily lives for many years to come lest we end up more like Lombardy than Veneto.

Key Points

1. Pandemics are fundamentally a problem of a lack of knowledge regarding who is infected and who has been infected. With that knowledge, we can isolate the infected and release the immune. Without that knowledge, physical interactions are unsafe.

2. Being able to conduct tests of whether people have or had COVID-19 will be critical to a faster opening-up of the economy and a restoration of economic and social life.

3. Moving to a testing economy is the way of making workers safe, and tests need not be perfect in order for this to occur.

4. Countries and regions that were able to test, trace, and then isolate the infected were able to contain the virus quickly and reopen their economies sooner.

8
Keeping It to Yourself

AIDS continues to be a major global calamity (with nearly one million deaths each year). This is despite the availability of effective treatments. Thanks to antiretroviral therapy (ART), the symptoms of AIDS can be reversed, lives are prolonged by decades, and even the infectiousness of HIV (the virus that causes AIDS) can be diminished. And this medication is now freely available globally. Nonetheless, it seems that some people at risk avoid being tested to see if they may need this treatment.

The number one reason why is the stigma associated with HIV/AIDS. If others believe that you might be a potential carrier of HIV, you may be rejected as a potential sexual partner. Now you might think, therefore, that getting tested would help. The problem is that even getting a test may send a social signal that you are the sort of person who may be riskier. In a close-knit community, it is difficult to conceal your actions (unlike elsewhere where medical visits can be undertaken more privately). Hence, due to a lack of privacy, people may opt not to know. The lack of testing leads to more infections and less treatment. For instance, in villages in Malawi, Africa, HIV testing rates were low, but of the little that was done, a third involved people traveling to other villages for tests. This was consistent with a privacy concern that social observation of testing would cause individuals some social harm.

Researchers Laura Derksen, Adamson Muula, and Joep van Oosterhout examined this possibility by conducting an experiment in public information dissemination in Malawi.[1] They held public information sessions about ART, and for the control group, they emphasized only the private benefits, while for the treatment group, they also emphasized the ability of ART to reduce the infectiousness of HIV by 96 percent. The intervention led to a small (one third) but significant increase in HIV testing and also seemed to affect nearby testing. This mirrored earlier analyses that showed that giving monetary incentives for HIV tests worked because they obscured the purpose of people visiting clinics.[2] It is all well and good to make testing available, but when it comes to infectious diseases, we should not take for granted that testing will be used or the results of such tests will be freely disclosed.

Public health was always going to be the place where the desire for privacy and the need for information on individuals would collide. There is strong evidence that more stringent privacy regulations—especially ones that raise privacy concerns without specifics—harm the adoption of electronic medical records systems and genetic testing.[3] This is particularly costly as such adoption has demonstrable health outcomes. For instance, Amalia Miller and Catherine Tucker found that when more births occur in hospitals that have adopted electronic medical record systems, neonatal fatalities drop (i.e., a 10 percent shift in electronic medical record adoption in a location leads to a reduction of 16 deaths per 100,000 live births in the United States).[4]

As has been the theme of this book, managing public health, especially with regard to the control of infectious diseases, requires good information, particularly for individual cases. But, at the same time, people have a high regard for control over information about their own health status. While studies have shown that people will happily give their own personal information (e.g., name, contact information, address) for as little as a slice of pizza,[5] health information, as the AIDS discussion above demonstrates, is another matter. Your health tells others how safe you are to be around and so it is not surprising people want to control those signals. When you combine that with infection control methods like contact tracing, it is easy to see why, even with tests and other methods available, public health officials may find it difficult to procure the information they need.

The basic principle remains, however, that for public health the more information that can be collected and utilized, the better. However, this will be possible only if people feel safe in providing that information, which requires doing everything possible to minimize privacy concerns. The alternative is mandating information collection, something that is both imperfect and leads to other consequences such as people concealing their behavior or avoiding revealing information for fear of where that information might end up.

This chapter will highlight the problems associated with getting people to get tested and with allowing public health officials access to other information they might need. At its core, people have an individual incentive to keep information private while the information itself could, if disclosed, help others. There are methods that allow privacy to be preserved, but no method is perfect; thus, procuring information will remain a difficult task.

Testing and Isolation

Knowing who is infected is the most valuable type of information we could have to control the spread of COVID-19. HAVE tests tell us whether someone is safe to be around. But the upshot is that to be effective, that information has to come with a consequence:

someone who tests positive needs to be isolated. This may not simply be isolation at home but within the home, or, to be most effective, isolated in a place away from home with other infected individuals.[6] None of these options is a picnic. All of them involve costs being imposed on the infected individuals.

On the positive side, even if a test results in isolation, people may be willing to accept that if that isolation increases the probability that they could be treated early and avoid graver risks.[7] However, with so many asymptomatic with COVID-19 and never developing into more serious health concerns, there may be a temptation to wait and see rather than disrupt their own lives with isolation. People who know a positive test leads to quarantine may avoid having a test in the first place in order to avoid the costs associated with isolation.

The natural potential solution that arises here is to allow people to obtain tests and then to voluntarily disclose the results or go into isolation. But there is a sense in which this is potentially worse. Prior to a test, one of the things causing you to engage in social distancing is the risk of becoming infected. If you have a positive test, that risk disappears. Even though the risk to others has increased, a purely self-interested person will take fewer precautions that would have reduced the chance of infecting many others. This could actually lead to an increase in the rate of infection among the population; precisely the opposite of what testing was intended to achieve.[8] This suggests that alongside testing, it is better to have mandatory quarantine even if this makes people less motivated to obtain tests in the first place.

How do you motivate people to obtain tests? The natural economic solution is to pay them. Indeed, it has been calculated that the social benefits of isolating an infected individual may be $2,000 per week, which suggests a substantial scope for a mutually beneficial arrangement between individuals and society.[9] One possibility is to match testing incentives with social distancing choices. For instance, those who stay at home may receive a test and a bonus payment if they test positive, while those who go to work are tested there and receive a bonus if they test negative. In this way, people sort themselves on the basis of their own assessed risk of being infectious and bear the costs or reap the benefits associated with their decision as the case may be.[10]

Knowing Where You Have Been

Given that testing is unlikely to be comprehensive, public authorities are likely going to have to gather relevant information in other ways. A common method, as outlined in the previous chapter, is contact tracing. This involves recording the history of travel of infected individuals to identify whom they may have come in contact with and target further investigations there. In this, information is revealed not simply about someone's health status but about their movements and meetings as well. Once again, this is something many people may want to keep private.

Knowing where people have been becomes useful when it is established that a person has been infected with the coronavirus. The information you want is a detailed description of that person's movements including where they went and how long they were in a particular location. Then you would want to match that with similar information from other people so that you could identify those who had contact with the individual, where that contact was (e.g., indoors or outdoors), how close the contact was, the duration of the contact, and, finally, whether any of the individuals was wearing protective gear or not. From this information you could assess the likelihoods that the infection may have spread to others and then target them for testing and isolation.

While testing can identify a particular individual who is infected and can isolate them, the advantage of using tracing as well is that you might be able to preemptively quarantine the next wave of infected individuals while you take the time to test them and verify their health. This is especially useful in situations where tests might not otherwise be sought unless symptoms appear. Tracing, used in this way, puts you one step ahead of the virus in the information game.

There are different ways that this type of information can be gathered. The traditional method was given the term "dirty boots epidemiology" whereby contact tracers interviewed an infected person about their movements and then put together a list of contacts and then interviewed them. The difficulty here is obvious in that it may be difficult to identify some individuals, let alone track them down quickly. However, the personal touch may make it easier to identify individuals with whom an infected person had more intensive contact and to use those social connections to extract more of the necessary information. The type of action taken will depend on the nature of the contact, with more intense contacts isolated (kept somewhere away from their homes and family) and monitored (with regular medical check-ins) and less intense ones asked to quarantine (be asked to stay in their homes).

Interviews rely on people being willing to disclose their travels. However, it is not hard to imagine situations where people might fear issues associated with that information being disclosed. For instance, someone may not want to expose a relationship—personal or otherwise—they might be having, which would be a direct conflict with the entire purpose of contact tracing. This privacy issue may result in unreliable or, more likely, incomplete information. Thus, some countries have moved to supplement interviews with other information to make up for the possibility that people might keep their activities private. For instance, South Korea uses CCTV camera footage and also credit/debit card usage information to assist in identifying movements and contacts. In some cases, this may allow contact tracers to accelerate how quickly they can gather information. It also allows interviewers to refresh the memories of those who are infected.

Given the potentially sensitive nature of this information, a key question is what happens to that information once it is collected.

In South Korea, the information is made public. While names are not used, the data on locations where an infected person was is made available on an app. This allows people to check their own mobility information with that on the app to see if they are at increased risk. But, at the same time, once that match occurs, the information is no longer necessarily private as the individuals concerned might be able to recognize each other. People no longer have high control over their health status information and, thus, that might make them less willing to provide that information in the first place.

These issues potentially become more salient when governments turn to other ways of tracking and recording locations. GPS tracking of mobile phones can potentially indicate where their users are or have been. That information, when provided to public health authorities, can be used to trace contacts. It is also useful to track potential outbreaks and other population-level measures of compliance with health guidance or laws. For instance, Google (through GPS tracking), Apple (through Maps usage), and SafeGraph (using data acquired at businesses and points of interest) all provide aggregated data on the movements of people. This has been useful, for instance, in establishing that much social distancing occurs regardless of whether there is a mandated and enforced lockdown or not. However, once this information is used to identify individual histories, the privacy issues rise again to the fore.

For this reason, another approach based on proximity detection has been developed. This uses Bluetooth on smart phones to identify other people (well, really, phones) that have been proximate to you for more than a certain period of time. If you turn out to be infected, the solution that many apps and also the efforts of Apple and Google have involves you then sending information regarding your contacts to a central point whereby that information can be used to notify those with whom you have had contact and to recommend a course of action (such as asking you to obtain a test or to self-quarantine).

An important problem with proximity detection is that it takes two to tango. A proximity event requires both people to have smart phones with the relevant app/service turned on. In the United States, only 81 percent of the population have a smart phone, which means that the best you can hope for is recording 65 percent of events. If only 40 percent have the app, that probability is down to 20 percent. Thus, the information is helpful but not comprehensive.

This means that officials need to be extra-sensitive to anything that might cause individuals not to adopt such tracing apps. Proximity systems can be set up so that only the individuals concerned are notified of risky contacts. Thus, they have the potential to provide information but, at the same time, give people control over how that information is used. Nonetheless, there remains the issue that in this case you have given the decision as to whether to disclose that information to individuals who have to balance their own privacy with any public health benefits. For some governments, concern over that balance has led them to take the decision out of individuals' hands. The information is shared automatically with public health officials, which, of course, magnifies those privacy concerns. This may lead individuals to avoid ways of collecting that information entirely. Indeed, in Singapore where such public health officials did obtain information from apps, the adoption of the app was very low.

The Bottom Line

The key takeaway from this chapter is that privacy concerns that limit the disclosure of information to public health officials can make it much harder to manage the COVID-19 pandemic. Economists studied South Korea's information disclosure practices during the crisis.[11] Their analysis of the flow of people through different areas found that having public disclosure of locations likely saved the country 400,000 cases and 13,000 fatalities compared with a situation where that information was not disclosed. In other words, South Korea was able to avoid a lockdown that took place in other countries precisely because they had the information they needed to manage the pandemic.

That said, the more that potential privacy concerns can be addressed (through increased security or management by a trusted partner), the better the adoption of apps that disclose important information will be. Of course, like location tracking, proximity detection can still potentially allow someone you had contact with to identify that it was you who was infected. There is also a myriad of other potential security risks that could still arise (e.g., a bad actor using a false infection to target contacts in a given place to shut it down—like a bomb threat). No method is perfect, but with careful management those risks can be minimized.

Key Points

1. Privacy concerns may stand in the way of both testing and contact tracing and, thus, impair the ability of public health officials to gather information to manage the pandemic.

2. People will weigh their need for information to manage their own health risks against the potential costs they see associated with their privacy.

3. Those costs can result in social ostracism, a change in social status, or a loss in social opportunities. Thus, individuals would be more likely to collect information if they have control over whom that information is disclosed to.

4. It is important, therefore, to build in privacy protections to ensure that information, when disclosed, is being put only to its intended use and minimizes the risk of disclosure to others.

9

Reemergence

In 2009, an Australian epidemiologist who had moved to Canada (giving me certain affinity with him), Professor Robert Smith?,[1] captured some interest by considering the best methods by which the world could ward off a zombie outbreak. Zombies are, to the best of our knowledge, infected humans who are technically dead but—what is relevant here—are still infectious, passing the problem to others by biting them. The resulting mathematical model showed that the way to deal with a zombie outbreak is to stamp it out quickly in one big, determined push. This yielded some support from Neil Ferguson, who would go on to coauthor the influential Imperial report for the COVID-19 crisis.[2]

> My understanding of zombie biology is that if you manage to decapitate a zombie then it's dead forever. So perhaps they are being a little over-pessimistic when they conclude that zombies might take over a city in three or four days.[3]

My understanding from this is that Ferguson thought that lopping off a zombie's head was a pretty straightforward approach, and that was the end of the matter. Nonetheless, the US Centers for Disease Control and Prevention put up a website to inform the public just in case.[4]

Viral pandemics are similar to zombie infestations in two respects. First, they both attack humans, and second, they move from human to human. Where they differ is that viruses can be killed proactively (through antiviral treatments) or passively by eventually either killing or dying out in a host. (Zombies can be killed only via decapitation.) The problem with viruses, as was already discussed in the previous chapter, is the lack of knowledge regarding who is or has been infected. With zombies, it is plain as day.

The upshot of this relatively invisible enemy is that the management strategy for a viral pandemic is likely to be ongoing and its end hard to measure or be sure of. In principle, there are actions that could be taken to suppress COVID-19 in one go. Moreover, suppression requires 100 percent success, and unless knowledge is available very quickly, the type of containment strategy one might use for a zombie situation is not warranted. This means that pandemic management requires an approach that will have to be actively conducted over many months. It will not be comfortably over in the course of a two-hour movie.[5]

In this chapter, I will examine reemergence strategies following initial isolation actions taken with regard to a pandemic. As has already been noted, isolation is economically and socially costly, and, as of the time of writing, it is reasonable to suspect that there will be immense political pressures to plan a path from isolation to reemergence while managing the pandemic and preventing future uncontained outbreaks. It is important to have a clear strategy because, in its absence, there may be pressures to let the virus "burn" through the population, creating herd immunity even with a massive loss of life.

The Cat Is out of the Bag

Before considering a reemergence strategy, it is worth reflecting on why that strategy is needed. The basic epidemiological goal is to move the basic reproduction number of the infection (R_0) to a point where it is less than one. In that situation, even an unmanaged virus will end up being contained and be on a path to dying out. As already emphasized, the issue is knowledge. If we know whether you HAVE or HAD COVID-19, and presuming that gives ongoing immunity, we can use individual-specific interventions to achieve that goal.

The benchmark is to consider what we could have done if we had that requisite knowledge from the outset. In that situation, we could continue to test and isolate those who tested positive. This would not be fun for those so identified, but it is better to isolate justifiably than indiscriminately.

The problem is that such knowledge is not available to even the most alert pandemic response teams. This means that the cat is out of the bag, and, thus, the virus is spreading, making it even harder to acquire the requisite knowledge. Indeed, it is precisely because of this that most countries (starting with China around Wuhan) had to pursue a widespread isolation or lockdown. This will eventually get the rate of infection down, but then what? After all, so long as there are still infected people somewhere, the basic reproduction number itself will not be below one (as too small a share of the population is immune), and the virus, in the absence of interventions, will likely reemerge.

The answer is that when the cat is out of the bag, first you have to put it back in the bag, and then you have to start over again. However, this time, the hope is that you have the capability to acquire knowledge to manage the spread of the virus in round two. In other words, all of the initial actions to contain the spread of the virus (including flattening the curve) are about getting to a point where you can have a "do over." That means evolving to a testing economy as described in the previous chapter. The question for reemergence is: Can we achieve a "do over" while at the same time allowing a relaxation of the policies surrounding initial containment?

Who's on First?

My starting point is a hypothetical country that has engaged in a widespread lockdown and has started to see signs that the rate of infection is starting to fall. At this point, it may be possible to predict when the infection rate falls below a level that would cause it to break out again. And before that point, there may be opportunities for a targeted and measured release of people from isolation.

The picture you should have in mind is that there is a set of activities in the economy, and, under containment, we have moved some activities from the unrestricted bucket to the restricted bucket. The question we need to ask ourselves is: When do we remove a given activity from the restricted to the unrestricted bucket? The answer from economics is that you want to move activities out of restrictions earlier if they have a high economic value and a low potential for increasing the spread of the virus. The ones that you want to delay are ones where there are few economic costs to the restriction and/or a large potential for causing the rate of infection to spread quickly.[6]

The question is: What first? The lockdown procedures in most places make a distinction between essential and nonessential work. Essential work is in healthcare, key public services, and food supply. For the most part, "essential" is a designation based on the value of their jobs rather than considerations of whether they were in jobs that may facilitate a faster spread of the virus. Indeed, healthcare work is a case in point, and hospitals, where possible, have put in place measures to stop the spread of the virus within those workplaces and beyond (with those workers being housed away from their homes in some cases).

The harder decisions will be for the nonessential work. There are two criteria that would guide this choice, based on the nonessential workers' economic value and potential to spread the virus. Let's begin with economic value. According to some studies, about 34 percent of the US workforce are in jobs that permit them to work from home.[7] If you work outdoors or work with specialized machinery, however, it is not likely you can work from home. But if you are doing legal, computer, or mathematical work, you do not actually need to be near anyone else to do your job. Thus, on an economic basis, it is reasonable to expect that construction and manufacturing work will rank highly as candidates for movement back from isolation.

The second criterion is on the basis of what types of activities and jobs would potentially pose a lower risk of spreading the virus.[8] In network theory, the issue is how connected people are to a broader network.[9] In modern societies, you can draw links between almost any two people. Those links are sometimes direct but usually indirect. A virus can potentially spread along those links, which is why it is commonplace to see outbreak data given on a country or maybe state basis. There are links between countries, but as fewer people travel between them, the "distance" along the network (in terms of number of people along a path) can potentially be greater.

But for reemergence we are starting from a situation where we have already broken the network. For a "stay in place" lockdown, this is almost to the level of individual households. Those households are components that link with each other. Every household has some members who venture out to obtain food or healthcare, and so, even though they are weaker, there are some links across households by this mechanism. When we take a household and allow members of that household to return to work, we are increasing the number of links between households.

You might think that means that if we allow one member of a household to return to work, we should allow other members to also do so. As that household will be integrated into the main economy with just one connection, why not have two? However, unless the members are literally going to the same place outside the household, additional household members being released magnifies the problem. Person A goes to their workplace and comes back potentially infected, which infects the household and also person B, who is going somewhere else. Having more links outside embeds the components (in this case, households) more densely in the network, which is what you want to avoid. This suggests that, where possible, at most one member of the household, initially, should be able to return to work.

This logic also explains why it is difficult to, say, remove an entire region from lockdown. In doing this, all of the households in a region become one component, and so if there is any incidence of the virus remaining, it will spread throughout. By contrast, if you take a more targeted release, even within a region, you can keep the basic reproduction factor low.[10]

The related point is that hubs need to be limited. A hub is a single location (which may, of course, also be a transportation conduit) where many people interact.[11] A candidate here is the central business district of a city but it also applies to schools and commuter colleges. The problem here is that if you open up a type of job, say, law firms, then, if they are located in the same place, you create the potential to spread the virus more quickly. This carries over to workplaces in general.[12] To keep the virus from spreading again, you have to limit the number of people in any given location. This means that workplaces need to be open but at a low scale. If they cannot operate in that way, it may be better for those workplaces to move to the back of the queue. This logic almost certainly applies to schools and colleges, which are hubs for interactions and also places where it is hard to use mitigating interventions such as good hygiene practices. It also almost certainly means that public events—sporting events, concerts, conferences, and elections—will not be able to take place as per normal for some time.[13]

This analysis suggests that among the first people to be allowed to return to work following isolation will be a subset of those people who cannot work from home. That subset will be determined by ensuring that if there are connections between what might be otherwise isolated groups (or components), those connections are sparse (meaning one or very few connections per person). Of course, this can be modified depending on the ability to use methods (preventative gear and cleaning) to ensure a lack of spread in workplaces and on transportation conduits.[14] At the time of writing, it is difficult to say who would make up that subset. However, one suspects construction and manufacturing will be high on the list, while schools and colleges may well be low. Schools will perhaps be the greatest challenge given their social importance (not to mention their role in general parental mental health, and their ability to allow parents to work from home without interruption or to work out of the home).

Suggestions have been made that the criterion for release should be based on whether a person is at risk from the serious complications from the coronavirus rather than their risk to others. For instance, it was suggested that younger members of the workforce be allowed to return to work.[15] The idea is that even if those groups end up spreading the virus among each other, there will not be serious health consequences relative to the economic value of them being allowed to work. However, risk to self is very different from the criteria of economic value and potential harm to others. Our confidence in doing this would depend on whether those groups would be sufficiently segregated from others as well as what the health effects might actually be. That said, absent a heavy hand in enforcement, as people are released, whether someone stops socially distancing or not is motivated by the assessment of their own risks. The question will then be whether to let what happens happen or to manage the difference between private and social incentives in some other manner.

Finally, it is useful to consider what might happen with regard to travel—not locally but regionally and internationally. At first blush, it seems that maintaining travel bans is an effective policy. After all, they keep the virus contained within countries.[16] However, as reemergence takes place, trade and travel will grow, consequently increasing the potential for the virus to leak through those boundaries. Given this and the economic importance of some travel, there seems no reason to single out those jobs for continued isolation. Instead, I suspect that, at least through airports, there will be more opportunities for testing (assuming fast tests are available) and also for the use of protective gear. Airports are already places where people have experience in dealing with frictions. The additional frictions that might be required may be relatively cheap from that perspective.

The above discussion focuses entirely on reducing the spread of the virus throughout reemergence. Another possibility is to focus on allowing reemergence subject to the constraint that those who are more vulnerable remain isolated from others. This is akin to the proposed policy of isolating the elderly and others with identifiably compromised immune systems who are most at risk from hospitalization or worse from COVID-19.[17] As a policy to introduce from scratch when people are not practicing social distancing, targeted isolation appeared difficult to achieve in practice. However, for reemergence, we may have more confidence that the virus is free in certain places. Therefore, as we allow movement to reemerge, we can continue to keep people isolated where there are identifiably higher risks, allowing connections only with certain precautions in place. If this were possible, then that would allow a greater number of people outside those groups to be able to operate more freely. Nonetheless, it is unclear at this stage whether we have the requisite knowledge to confidently pursue this approach of using "not at risk" as a criterion for targeted release.

Key Points

1. There will come a point where COVID-19 has been contained and governments will move to relax social distancing policies. However, as most of the population will not be immune, this will likely have to be a staged process.

2. The criteria for release will be a balance of economic importance as well as the likelihood of causing infections to spread. Large gatherings, such as sporting events, will be unlikely to return until the crisis is completely over.

3. Key to release will be the density of the workplace, the location away from central hubs, and the ability to enact workplace-level prevention policies. This will likely mean that people who cannot work from home will be higher on the list. The most challenging decision will come with respect to school openings.

4. Care will need to be taken with reopening to ensure that secondary outbreaks do not arise within specific communities or social circles. This will require every manager of a physical space becoming their own public health policy maker.

10

Rallying Innovation

This chapter is about how we can innovate our way out of this and future crises. Thus, it seems appropriate to begin with the movie *Mission Impossible 2*. Released in 2000, the antagonist is an Australian-based biotech company (Biocyte Pharmaceuticals, if you must know) with a rather unique commercialization plan. They have developed a virus, Chimera, that could start a very bad pandemic—it lies dormant for 20 hours before destroying the carrier's red blood cells. One plan might have been threatening to release the virus and being paid not to do so. But the folks at Biocyte went one step further. They planned to release the virus itself because they had also developed the cure. And because, of course, they hold the patent on it. I suspect some venture capitalists would call this one "fundable."

The movie plot involved the chase to stop the virus being released but also to secure the cure in case it was. But I wonder, did they have to? The plan was to release the virus and then charge for the cure. Drugs normally, once made available, are easy to copy and so have patents. So it appears that the plan here was to use the patent to extort world governments to pay up much of global wealth.

But herein lies the problem: the patent is granted by those governments. Surely in this situation, they would just invalidate the patent and take the cure?

The point—and you will see that I do have one—is that when it comes to innovations in the face of global pandemics, business as usual for our innovation system is unlikely to apply. The reason is that once an innovation has been created, there are strong pressures to make it freely available and, in the process, push down the return to any R&D that has been conducted. Anticipating this, businesses may not invest in R&D in the first place. And this is not a hypothetical situation.

> Such concerns are likely very salient to firms. For example, after Senator Paula Hawkins (R-FL) asked a major vaccine manufacturer how it could justify charging nearly three times as much to the U.S. government for vaccines as to foreign countries, U.S. manufacturers stopped submitting bids to UNICEF to supply vaccines. . . . When President Bill Clinton announced his plan to immunize all children against a standard list of diseases in 1993, he said, "I cannot believe that anyone seriously believes that America should manufacture vaccines for the world, sell them cheaper in foreign countries, and immunize fewer kids as a percentage of the population than any nation in this hemisphere but Bolivia and Haiti." . . . In the face of such statements, potential risks facing firms seem real.[1]

It is very unlikely that governments around the world are going to accept monopoly pricing for a vaccine developed for COVID-19 that potentially will benefit 7 billion people. For life-saving drugs, it is not uncommon for those prices to be in the hundreds of thousands per person. For a vaccine intended to be given to a population such as that of the United States, even $10,000 per dose would set the government back $3 trillion. That is not going to happen.

Will governments likely pay a princely sum for a vaccine for COVID-19? Yes. Will it cover the costs and the risks associated with developing and trialing that vaccine? Hopefully. But given the uncertainty amid the crisis, there is a concern that pharmaceutical companies and their researchers do not need to add further uncertainty. Moreover, this isn't just about the current crisis. Like the flu, coronaviruses are probably with us for the foreseeable future and may require annual vaccine development. There are other innovations (e.g., methods to test and anticipate pandemics) that we might finally demand, having felt the costs of a global pandemic in the modern era. All of those will be of a public nature with the idea of using them widely. That means that the price for these innovations will be set in negotiation with governments that, we can imagine, are unlikely to be less stingy with public funds for pandemic prevention going forward. Given this, how should we think about an innovation system for what are essentially ideas that will enhance the global public good?

The Pull of Demand

Before considering how we will rally information, it is important to note that one part of the system is working well: the crisis has generated demand for innovations that will mitigate the costs of the pandemic and also potentially end it. In studying innovation, there have been broad arguments regarding how strong the pull of demand is in spurring the direction of innovative activity. The chief proponent that demand-pull was critically important was Jacob Schmookler, who documented that patent records showed that new needs drove the types of innovations we saw.[2]

Part of this innovation effort has been directed toward making places safer in terms of spreading infection. Alberto Galasso and Hong Luo have documented many cases in the current crisis where the increased awareness of risks has spurred new innovations.[3] For instance, large call centers in China quickly innovated in security

a) Therapies pipelines

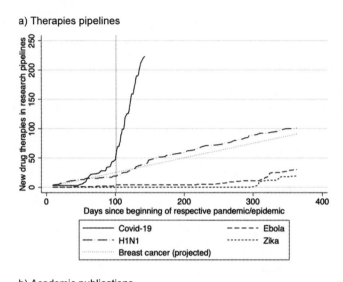

b) Academic publications

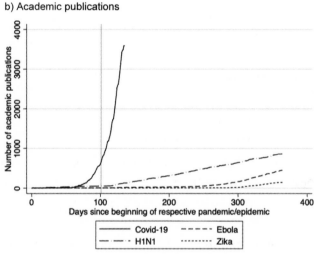

Figure 10.1
(a) Therapies pipeline. (b) Academic publications. *Source:* Kevin A. Bryan, Jorge Lemus, and Guillermo Marshall, "Innovation during a Crisis: Evidence from Covid-19," mimeo., University of Toronto, (April 29, 2020): figure 1.

and IT systems to allow workers to operate from home with 20–40 percent likely to continue to do so even as the economy reopens. As it turns out, changes in risk perceptions have been an important driver of innovations in the past.[4]

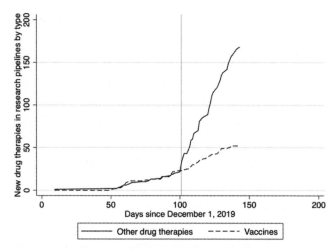

Figure 10.2
Research into therapies versus vaccines. *Source:* Kevin A. Bryan, Jorge Lemus, and Guillermo Marshall, "Innovation during a Crisis: Evidence from COVID-19," mimeo., University of Toronto, April 29, 2020, figure 2.

While this makes intuitive sense, it is also often the case that we need scientific breakthroughs to generate ideas for new innovations. Economists have also examined how the onset of the crisis changed research as indicated by scientific publications.[5] Figure 10.1 compares the COVID-19 pipeline for new drug therapies in pharmaceutical research with those of Ebola, Zika, and H1N1and also the volume of disease-related research articles in academic journals. As can be seen, the shift in research emphasis is dramatic even compared with previous crises. Figure 10.2 examines the focus on vaccine development and shows a similar dramatic effect.

While this indicates that science has moved quickly in response to COVID-19, we have to be mindful that the acid test for innovation is the speed with which prospects can be found to actually work (rather than just explored), found to be safe (without unintended consequences), and then actually delivered to market. It is with these final steps that we have to be concerned that the system will work.

Why Traditional Innovation Incentives Won't Cut It

The usual way we try to encourage innovation in a market economy is to reward the innovator with intellectual property protection. If you have a new drug, you can secure a patent that gives you the exclusive right to sell it for about 15 years. In other words, your reward is to make whatever profits you can for a time unimpeded by close competition. That system works pretty well.[6] However, the main problem with regard to innovations that will help avoid or stem the effects of a global pandemic is a contradiction—in order for the innovator to receive profits, we have to allow the innovator to price in such a way that many will be unable to use the innovation. As our goal is widespread use, this contradiction is prohibitive.

The difficulty for a vaccine maker is that a low price on the vaccine reduces their profits but generates much more value for other firms as the economy recovers. There are clever ideas, however, to help the vaccine maker recover some of this value. Consider this, as told by columnist Matt Levine:

> [I]f I ran one of the big index-fund companies, and a pharmaceutical company in my portfolio developed a patented fully effective cure for Covid-19 that it could manufacture cheaply and planned to sell to anyone who could pay $50,000 a dose, I would call that company right up and say "no, you give that pill away for free, because the value to me of Covid-19 going away quickly and the economy recovering—the value to me as an owner of airlines and hotels and chain restaurants and retailers and every other company—is vastly, vastly greater than the value to me of your profits on that pill."[7]

This is pretty ingenious.[8] If you know you have a COVID-19 vaccine, then you know that, when it is released, there will be an economic boom and so you can invest in the stock market on the basis of that information. That should generate a healthy return. Unfortunately, it also requires a very large amount of capital to make the return that would incentivize the innovator. Relying on stock market processes to fund important innovative endeavors is risky at best.

Given the value on the table, the other option is to ignore the market altogether and have the government offer grants and subsidies to defray the costs of conducting research and development. This has certainly been a hallmark of the system of scientific research conducted in most countries following World War II.[9] The challenge is that it is very difficult to evaluate whether grants are being spent in an efficient manner. Consequently, grants tend to be favored where no other sources of funding are available—for instance, for basic research that has no commercial payoff and a high degree of uncertainty—or where there is expertise to evaluate the efficacy of the research program and required expenditures. This latter task, however, is itself not amenable to a quick disbursement of funds. Thus, if there is any urgency, such as lives being lost while research is being conducted, grants are unlikely to be an efficient means of generating innovations.

The Vaccine Challenge

And there is urgency. It is estimated that globally there is the equivalent of $375 billion being lost monthly as a result of COVID-19's depression on economic activity.[10] Thus, not only are there substantial economic benefits to developing a coronavirus vaccine, but there are substantial benefits to accelerating development and production of the vaccine.[11]

As already noted, there is already substantial scientific effort being put into developing candidate vaccines. The chances that any one of them is effective and safe for use is very low. Nonetheless, the fact that so many prospects are being explored suggests that there is a high likelihood that one of them at least will be safe and effective. The problem is that for any potential vaccine candidate, trials must be conducted before it is deemed safe for us and can be manufactured.

There are two broad ways to accelerate the time from creating a potential vaccine candidate to having it widely available for actual use. First, you can accelerate the speed of trials. Vaccine trials are typically undertaken by taking two large groups of people and giving one the vaccine and the other a placebo and then seeing if infection rates differ between the two groups (with the hope that one group will be largely immune) and also whether there are any other side effects from the vaccine. This can take years, especially if there are low rates of infection in the population. For this reason, some have advocated the use of challenge trials for vaccine development. Such trials would give the vaccine to healthy subjects who would either be paid or volunteer to be exposed to the coronavirus. If the vaccine works, that is great news for everyone. If not, then the volunteer will become infected and may consequently suffer health consequences. Suffice it to say, this is risky, not as scientifically valid, and, in ordinary times, not considered ethically defensible. As Alex Tabarrok argues, however, these are not ordinary times.[12] In emergencies, all manner of people volunteer for risky jobs like firefighting or, indeed, being a health worker during a pandemic. This practice accelerated the development of an Ebola vaccine in 2014.

The second way to accelerate time to market is to build manufacturing capability quickly. However, the problem is that for each vaccine candidate that enters trials, many of the elements of production require very different manufacturing plants. For this reason, Bill Gates proposed to accelerate the process, when a candidate enters trials, by building a plant to manufacture it. Critically, for vaccines, it is usually the case that you must build a distinct plant to manage production depending on the type of vaccine and cannot just repurpose a plant that is, say, making a vaccine for chicken pox, to switch to one for the novel coronavirus. Because of this, Gates proposed to build six or seven plants ahead of trials with the expectation that only one or two would prove useful and the rest would be mothballed. However, even with this, it is likely that 15 candidates need to be explored in order to minimize the likelihood that they all do not work out.[13] This is even beyond Gates's pocketbook, and, thus, other mechanisms are needed if manufacturing capacity is going to be built in this way.

One part of this would be to use international cooperation. This would allow plants to be built in different countries but also for governments to coordinate efforts on critical bottleneck components such as glass vials that are needed to transport the vaccine to people. For instance, the United States is a net importer of most such supplies so that even if they built manufacturing capacity for a candidate, they would need to rely on global production to produce any vaccine. Thus, there are gains to cooperation prior to a vaccine being developed, but cooperation also will be important afterward, with some countries more at risk from restrictions on exports that might accompany nation-prioritization of doses. Given that it is unknown where a vaccine will be developed and where the components to produce it will come from, there are substantial benefits to countries agreeing on a process for the distribution of those components and eventual doses before the fact.[14] The place to start would be to divide up the estimated cost of $145 billion in measures designed to bring vaccines to market quickly.

Advanced Market Commitments

Given that grants can go only so far to accelerate vaccine provision, economists have considered alternative ways of encouraging innovations by private businesses. These combine the elements of grants with market signals. One approach contemplated was the use of prizes. For centuries, benefactors have announced prizes that would be paid in the event certain inventions were generated. The most famous was the prize for a device that measured longitude at sea so as to provide a dramatic improvement in maritime navigation.[15]

Prizes have the advantage that they are clearly solutions to problems someone believes it would be valuable to solve.[16] Thus, they have a market signal embedded in their makeup. The difficulty is that the problems that are usually specified are to achieve some scientific milestone such as proving a mathematical theorem or landing a spacecraft on the moon. These are not necessarily of the class that would require widespread adoption for the global public good. For pandemics and pandemic control, we are talking about inventions whose adoption will impact billions of people. Thus, quality and workability really matter. They cannot simply be scientific advances. The innovations need to be able to work for their intended function. That is a tougher challenge than any one prize for a significant milestone is likely to achieve.[17]

To solve these problems and enhance the market test associated with prize-like mechanisms, Michael Kremer proposed the use of advanced market commitments (AMCs).[18] Suppose you are trying to encourage the development and then manufacture of a vaccine. An AMC is a contract without a specific counterparty that a donor/sponsor offers to deliver the intended vaccine. The contract specifies that the provider (as yet unknown) will be guaranteed a certain payment per dose of the vaccine up to a specified number of doses. This serves to set a floor on what the provider might earn because the contract specifies a subsidy for every dose actually purchased. So, a country, for instance, may pay a low price (such as $1) per dose but the provider would receive an additional subsidy (say, $15) per dose. Thus, there is a guaranteed payoff for providers, but, in return, providers agree to cap the price they charge for the vaccine. Their overall earnings are greater the more doses are actually sold. Obviously, if there are no candidates that pass certain quality standards, the contract is never paid out.

A key feature of AMCs is that they are not compulsory. Recall that the reason we need AMCs that "stick" for innovations that potentially have high social value is that, in their absence, governments and other donors may claw back on promised returns. Thus, it is important that AMCs are a strong commitment. If AMCs are non-compulsory, then any innovator could choose to sell their product at whatever price they choose if they do not accept the AMC. A compulsory AMC only enhances rather than reduces the returns to any R&D investments. The commitment increases the price above what the market would pay, and, thus, the AMC contains a prize-like element but only if the vaccine is used by lots of people.

How could AMCs be deployed for pandemic-related innovations? It depends on some features of the innovation—specifically, how close current efforts are to a viable product. For innovations that are more technologically distant, the goal is to encourage more R&D effort and resources. This might be the case for a vaccine that could handle most potential coronaviruses as opposed to the specific virus that is currently spreading. The challenge in designing the AMC is setting a price that will induce that R&D effort. This will be an easier task if that price encourages multiple simultaneous attempts to pursue the innovation. At the same time, however, AMC designers will want to ensure that innovators' payoffs are sensitive to how well their products work, so they push innovation toward products that are likely to be more effective. Thus, even though the price might be set ex ante, to encourage that effort and align incentives, AMCs for technologically distant innovations will likely remove the floor (in terms of sales guarantees) to give innovators more "skin in the game."

For COVID-19, as already noted, the likely place an AMC could be deployed is to accelerate vaccine development and production. With a number of candidate prospects in the pipeline,[19] the chief constraint is not riskier R&D but instead undertaking trials and then building capacity to bring these products to market. An AMC designer faces a challenge as they would not have accurate information regarding the costs of those activities even if they know they are potentially substantial. The good news is that they have better information regarding precisely what the potential prospects can achieve.

In setting the per unit price for the AMC, for a technologically close product, the designer has to refrain from setting a very low price—even though that may save on overall costs to those using the innovation—and err on the side of a higher price so that the necessary capacity investments actually are made.[20] As there is likely urgency in getting products to market quickly, you would not want to skimp on payments and risk insufficient capacity. Again, this highlights the importance of the AMC's role as a commitment because, having built capacity, there will be pressures to reduce price. The AMC needs to guard against those pressures.

One thing that can take the pressure off prices in this situation is if the AMC can guarantee a certain level of sales for the product. After all, the innovator will be making investments depending on the overall return. Thus, they will be happy to trade off price for quantity so long as the total revenue (that is, price times quantity) does not change. This is a luxury that AMC designers have when setting terms of a technologically close product, as they have a much better sense of the overall level of demand for that product.

A relatively technologically close AMC has recently been undertaken to produce a pneumococcal conjugate vaccine specifically targeting developing countries where 700,000 children are estimated to die from the disease each year. Five countries and the Gates Foundation put up $1.5 billion for an AMC in 2007 and it was launched in 2009. Businesses would compete for a contract to supply the vaccine over a 10-year period with a price capped at $3.50 per dose (much lower than prices paid in developed countries) and a subsidy from the AMC of another $3.50 per dose.[21] In

2010, pharmaceutical companies GSK and Pfizer committed to each supply 30 million doses annually (a substantial fraction of the total need of 200 million). This vaccination campaign appears broadly successful, although we can never be completely sure what would have happened in the AMC's absence. Experience tells us that it likely would have been very little.

Given this, it is not surprising that economists Susan Athey, Michael Kremer, Christopher Snyder, and Alex Tabarrok have proposed using an AMC to develop a coronavirus vaccine.[22] They propose, for the United States at least, committing to a purchase of 300 million doses of a vaccine at $100 per dose. If there are multiple candidates at the same time, the contract would be awarded to the vaccine based on its ease of manufacture or suitability for a wide variety of demographic groups. Thus, businesses would compete for the contract but also to be of higher quality than others.

More Failure, Please!

Thus far, the discussion here has focused on why business as usual in terms of market and private rewards for innovation is unlikely to be suitable for pandemic-related innovations. However, there is also a sense in which governments, in particular, need to abandon business as usual that often accompanies their own funding on research and development—they are averse to failure.[23]

The innovation challenge is so potentially large that it is very important that we pursue as many different paths as possible. In a sense, there may be very important scientific and innovation directions out there, in which each has unclear and hard to understand potential payoffs. In other words, there is considerable uncertainty. The classic example was the development of the *Spitfire* fighter plane by the British just before World War II. The plane was faster and more maneuverable than anything before and had seemed implausible when it received funding in the 1930s. Winston Churchill opposed it. However, it arguably was instrumental in protecting Britain from invasion, as Churchill would later endorse.[24]

Given that the payoffs potentially can be very high, this suggests that we should be more comfortable pursuing riskier and potentially unconventional scientific approaches. In other words, there is a broad need for a portfolio approach to innovation—spreading our options widely—so as to better understand which paths might prove to be feasible.

The takeaway here is that governments and donors should not be afraid of casting their net very widely and funding not just moonshots but also loon-shots.[25]

A New Manhattan Project

In the midst of World War II, Franklin D. Roosevelt authorized the creation of a highly funded project to build the first nuclear bomb. The Manhattan Project was a stunning success. It brought together a workforce of 129,000 to the New Mexico desert, including a large concentration of scientists (three of whom had won and three of whom would later win Nobel Prizes), at a cost of what today would be $23 billion and, in three years, had built a working weapon. That weapon would create a decades-long existential crisis for the whole of humanity, causing fear and sowing mistrust that continues to this very day, but right now we can marvel at the fact that the project met all of its KPIs and ended World War II in relatively short order.

It is not a stretch to suggest that both managing the current COVID-19 pandemic (with tests, antivirals, and a vaccine) and coming up with innovations to more effectively manage future pandemics, a project well in excess of the scale of the Manhattan Project, is warranted.[26] Some proposals have included the potential to develop a platform for the almost routine development of vaccines as new threats emerge.[27] Based on the potential future economic cost alone, there is an easy rate of return justification. What is more, unlike the Manhattan Project, this would not have to be conducted with secrecy; indeed, there would be considerable merit to precisely the opposite in terms of openness.

This is not the place to scope out what that potentially massive endeavor would look like. However, I can list here some key features that should be considered as part of it:

- *International cooperation*: All of these efforts are in terms of contributing to a global public good. The challenge will be to find mechanisms that distribute the costs of achieving these goals in a workable and sustained manner.

- *Regulatory audit*: Each country should pursue a major regulatory audit to ensure that there are no unnecessary impediments to being able to innovate and then to adopt new promising technologies. The COVID-19 crisis has already led to a relaxing of some regulatory rules specifically regarding approvals for public drug release. For instance, the US Food and Drug Administration has fast-tracked various treatments and vaccine trials.

- *Patent pools*: There is merit to pooling together patents associated with COVID-19 and other future pandemic threats. A patent pool is an agreement between patent holders to licensing terms for patents between them. By agreeing to these, it is easier to combine innovations together to build products and services.[28] An example of this emerged during the COVID-19 crisis when a patented HIV therapy, Kaletra, was potentially promising as a treatment for the virus. The patent holder, Abbvie, announced it would not defend its patent rights.[29] A more formalized agreement before the fact regarding licensing would remove frictions even further.

- *Expert review boards*: The research involved will likely be pursued following various promising paths. This happened with the Manhattan Project where two different bomb designs were designed in parallel. It also happened after the war with the National Defense Research Committee.[30] To organize these competing streams, expert review boards will likely need to be constituted on an ongoing basis. This could assist in the allocation of funds, the highlighting of impediments, the evaluation of project quality, and the design of AMCs.

There is one thing a crisis of this magnitude should tell us: there is room to do better. The funding for innovation for medical research is a fraction of that devoted to other threats—notably, national security.[31] Our experience in 2020 suggests that our attention has been misfocused.

What about Pressing Needs?

Before leaving this topic entirely, it is useful to emphasize that the above considerations are focused on the public health innovations that are desperately required—that is, innovations that make it easier to treat or prevent COVID-19 and future pandemics. But there is another dimension of innovative activity that has more urgency but without the commitment concerns that usually govern health-directed innovations, that is, facilitating the recovery from the current crisis. Thus, it is useful to reflect on the nature of innovations for more pressing needs and how businesses should consider the opportunities presented in this regard.

Recall from chapter 9, that, at present, activities are placed in two buckets: restricted and unrestricted. To ensure speedier economic recovery, our goal is to move activities from the restricted to the unrestricted bucket. To minimize the ongoing economic costs, however, we would like the activities that are placed in the restricted bucket to have lower cost associated with being in that bucket. Thus, we can see that there are two broad classes of innovations that will be valuable over the next year.

First, there are innovations that reduce the potential for an activity that is currently restricted to generate too high an increase in potential COVID-19 infections. This would be innovations in protection at work, safety on public transport, and, what is likely to happen, a major investment by fashion designers in face-mask couture.

Second, there are innovations that are designed to make it easier to conduct activities that are restricted. This would, of course, include work-from-home tools such as video conferencing but also investments that may reduce the need for people to be physically present at work in general, such as the use of robots and automation. The latter innovations may simply be the acceleration of recent technological trends.

What is important to note about both of these potential innovative opportunities is that their value depends critically on bad news.[32] This might seem to be a rather grim thought for innovation but that does not make it less true. If you are moving quickly to develop an innovation that either reduces the infection possibilities from releasing an activity from restrictions or makes it easier to cope with restrictions, if it turns out that we have good news regarding COVID-19—say, it is less infectious, can be controlled with weaker economic restrictions, or is less dangerous to long-term health —then the economy may return to normal quickly. That will reduce the demand for any of the solutions that one of these innovations might present.

Nonetheless, while it is the case that our current innovative efforts have a return that is based on bad news—the virus turns out to have effects on the worse side of our expectations—the way to look at it is this: if it turns out that outcomes are good, then we can cheer from not having to hope for these innovations, while if they are bad, by making the attempt we have taken out some insurance cover. Overall, innovations will improve our prospective well-being.

Key Points

1. In pandemics, the usual way of rewarding innovative activity breaks down because governments and donors will put pressure on innovators to reduce price. Anticipating this, they may not invest in treatment, vaccines, or other innovations.

2. The need to commit to returns while ensuring wide dissemination of innovations means that advanced market commitments—contracts that provide pricing and volume guarantees prior to innovations being created—are worth being considered as a primary vehicle for globally relevant advances in knowledge.

3. The urgent nature of the crisis means that governments need to be failure-tolerant in pursuing a wide variety of approaches to solve a given problem.

4. The analogy for the innovative effort required is the Manhattan Project, which led quickly to the development of the atomic bomb and ended World War II. This implies devoting a substantial amount of resources to innovation in medicine and elsewhere to deal with COVID-19 as well as future pandemics.

11
The Big Rationing

Polio had ravaged the world for over five decades. A terrible disease that caused paralysis and death, primarily in children, polio was feared by all. In 1955, after decades of research, a safe vaccine produced in Jonas Salk's laboratory at the University of Pittsburgh had arrived. The US government sped it into production, but that rush was to prove costly. Manufacture the vaccine imperfectly, and it can turn from a suppressor into a spreader. For polio, one bad process led to 200 cases and 11 deaths.[1] With those tragic lessons learned, production was slowed. The result of this was that the vaccine would not be widely available. It would take years for vaccinations to be at a level at which the disease was effectively suppressed. Even then, cases still emerged through community transmission until 1979.

Experience and basic economics tell us that when a vaccine for the novel coronavirus is produced, we will not instantly end the pandemic. Instead, there will be a period of time—many months or a year—during which there will be a shortage of doses. As documented in the previous chapter, advanced market commitments acknowledge this and are used to build capacity quickly so that doses are readily available and life can return to normal quickly.

But, as of the time of writing, it is unclear how successful those efforts will be. Thus, it is natural to ask: What will happen if there are persistent shortages of the vaccine both within countries and worldwide?

Let's dismiss one option right away: the use of markets to allocate scarce doses. This might seem strange for an economist to say, but while markets do an excellent job of allocating scarce resources in normal circumstances, when it comes to products with high health consequences, market processes come up short in terms of driving outcomes that are generally thought of as socially equitable. Put simply, if your goal was to allocate vaccine doses to those who wanted them the most—in terms of what other purchases they would be willing to give up in order to obtain the vaccine sooner— markets can do a good job. If there are a limited number of doses that are allocated to the highest bidders, then people will bid up to their monetary value for a vaccine—including both health benefits and the ability to move around safely afterward. However, those values may be distorted if there are many people who simply do not have the money to be competitive in that bidding, that is, if they are wealth constrained. In this situation, it is unlikely that vaccines will be allocated to those who actually value them the most; instead, they will find their way to people who have money to spare. Thus, this is a situation where the economist's presumption that markets can deal with scarcity in an efficient manner cannot be presumed.[2] Fortunately, as we will see, most governments have understood this when it comes to health resources and have become accustomed to finding nonmarket ways of rationing scarce things.

Making a List

When it comes to vaccines, governments have anticipated that there may be shortages and have generated plans and protocols to allocate doses should they be scarce. The primary way this is done is to make a list of various groups of people who should receive priority and then, depending on availability, supply those higher up on that list first. This is something that is done by governments in other areas; for instance, many governments give priorities to work visas for people with desirable skills or who already have family members who have immigrated.

To take an example with respect to vaccines, the US CDC has five tiers of recipients for a typical flu vaccine.[3] There are two dimensions of priority: occupational groups (reflecting the earlier economic criteria) and high-risk populations (reflecting the at-risk criteria for harm from the virus). In tier 1 are the occupational groups who are already priorities for non-isolation during the containment phase today, including healthcare and security services. Tier 2 continues to include essential workers, especially with regard to infrastructure services, while the remainder of those are part of tier 3. Using the at-risk criteria, tier 1 includes pregnant women and babies; tier 2 expands that to high-risk children and people who work with young children; tier 3 includes the rest of children; tier 4 is high-risk adults; and tier 5 includes the rest. Notice that there are no occupational groups in tiers 4 and 5.

For COVID-19, the occupational group ordering makes sense and is in line with current practices regarding who is able to work as part of essential services. However, the at-risk ordering does not reflect what is currently understood about COVID-19, that is, that the older you are, the more at risk you are. The CDC guidelines take age into account when considering children. However, for COVID-19, it appears that the younger you are, the less at risk you are (although children may be vectors for disease spread). In other words, the guidelines for influenza, in general, do not reflect the realities of risk with respect to COVID-19. Thus, one would expect those to change. This will also generate a decision regarding healthy adults of working age and those who have retired. The latter are far more at risk, while for the former, there are economic criteria that will favor them. My point is to highlight this potential issue and suggest that there will be no easy decision in this regard.

What the criteria also do not reflect is any sense of network theory. For instance, prison populations are potentially risky areas where infections can break out. If testing was not available, there are arguments that they should receive priority for a vaccine.

Lotteries

Even looking beyond the use of guidelines to assign priority, there will be a large pool of people for whom there is a vaccine shortage but no identifiable way of prioritizing them. In that case, a lottery will likely be used (as it was in the movie *Contagion*).

A lottery randomly assigns available doses to people. In contrast to a market where it is likely that people who have both high valuations and high wealth will be vaccinated first, everyone has an equal chance for priority in a lottery. In particular, some people who have high valuations for the vaccine but low wealth will receive an allocation. Thus, a lottery reduces the wealth bias compared with markets but potentially at the cost of assigning vaccines to people who do not value them as urgently.

The idea of a lottery is to treat everyone equally. However, it may be, as was already discussed in the "list-making" approach to rationing, that there are classes of people whom you might like to give priority to and to have lotteries within those classes. For instance, you may decide that you want healthcare workers to receive allocations first and then others to receive their allocations via a lottery. In other cases, you might just want to prioritize healthcare workers but also give other people a potential allocation in a lottery—for instance, you may decide that you do not want all of the scarce doses being used by healthcare workers and want to leave some for others.

The choices of how to create those buckets for priority is not something about which an economist has special knowledge; it involves considerations of public health management, health risk, and ethical considerations. However, economists can point out that the details of how you operate such a system can matter.

For instance, suppose that you had 100 doses of a vaccine in a town. You decide that healthcare workers should receive a priority, but there are 100 of these people, so you want a system that reserves some doses for them but not all of them. Suppose you reserve half of the doses for healthcare workers and the rest are assigned by lottery to anyone (including healthcare workers) who remain. Suppose, just to make our mathematics easier, that there are 100 others in the town. In this situation, healthcare workers will receive 50 doses, and then, of the remaining 50 doses, other people will receive two thirds of them (as there are 100 other people among the 150 still to be vaccinated) and healthcare workers will receive one third. Thus, in the end, 67 healthcare workers receive doses.

Notice, however, that how you conduct this lottery matters. For instance, suppose you decided to reserve 50 doses for healthcare workers but only allocate them to those workers who miss out on the general lottery. In this case, half of those in the general lottery will likely be healthcare workers, and so 25 doses will be allocated to them in that stage. Then 50 more doses will be allocated afterward, bringing their total to 75. In other words, simply by reversing the stages—allocating generally before the specific reserve buckets— increases the number of healthcare workers who receive doses. The point here is that these two approaches look the same but have very different outcomes. Thus, depending on what you want to achieve in terms of actually prioritizing some group of people, you need to be sensitive to the procedure for allocation. Some economists have developed a procedure whereby people actually self-select into different priority categories as a way of signaling their own valuation in a quasi-market arrangement.[4]

Nonetheless, regardless of whether a lottery system or a list is used, there will be a decision that needs to be made regarding categories of people who might be given special priority or treatment as vaccine doses are rationed.[5]

Resale Markets

One possibility that arises when a lottery system is used to ration scarce resources is whether resale is allowed once someone has been assigned a dose in a lottery. While, at first blush, this might seem to undermine any desire to ensure that low wealth people receive doses sooner, it may be that everyone is better off by having this option.

Recall that one of the things that happen with a lottery is that some of those who have relatively low valuations for being vaccinated early win the lottery, while some who have high valuations miss out. In this case, there is an amount of money that someone with both high wealth and a high valuation is willing to part with to receive a dose that is greater than an amount that would persuade someone with a low valuation who won a lottery dose to part with theirs. As this latter trade is purely voluntary, it must be the case that both parties are better off for having the option. The end result is that more high valuation people actually receive doses independent of their wealth levels, and so this outcome is potentially superior to both a pure market and a pure lottery (without resale) allocation.[6]

Nonmonetary Signaling

Thus far, the methods of allocating scarce vaccine doses have relied on whether someone has wealth (a market process) or whether someone is a member of a category that is deemed to require priority. Otherwise, the doses are allocated using some random mechanism. But what if the fact that there is likely to be vaccine scarcity is used to create incentives for better behavior prior to that point in time? After all, we are asking people to engage in costly activities—most notably, socially distancing or being tested with a risk of being required to isolate—that perhaps some priority in getting vaccines might compensate for.

The notion that people might take some nonmonetary action to achieve priority when there is scarcity is not new. For instance, this happens when there is a new release of a limited supply product like Taylor Swift concert tickets or a new iPhone, and rather than prices rising, people are given the opportunity to queue up with the first people in line getting priority. While this can be a way of low wealth people signaling their high valuation, the queuing process itself is quite wasteful.[7]

Some economists realized that there might be ways to create a different type of market with respect to a treatment similar to a vaccine called convalescent plasma (CCP) therapy.[8] In this therapy, a patient who has recently recovered from COVID-19 donates blood to give to others in order to provide antibodies that can attack the novel coronavirus. This can serve as a treatment to help COVID-19 patients recover quickly. As CCP donations are scarce, it was suggested that if someone donates their plasma, then they might receive vouchers that they could assign to friends or family members to receive priority should they fall ill. In other words, the donor is "paid back" for their donation. Another way this could work is that someone who is already ill could commit to donating their plasma should they recover. In this way, they could "pay it forward" if they receive CCP therapy. These incentives could increase the supply of CCP donors.

One could imagine similar ways of "earning" vouchers for vaccines. For one, CCP donors could earn vouchers not just for CCP therapy for family members but for vaccines. More interestingly, if there were verifiable ways of measuring someone's social distancing, then they too could receive priority for vaccine allocations.[9] In other words, we could use the prospects of being able to receive a vaccine earlier as a way of encouraging more socially desirable behavior during the pandemic.

In the end, rationing is an important issue that will most likely arise. By planning early, we can make that process better, fairer, and potentially operate in a way that encourages good behavior. Regardless, what we should anticipate is a very fraught process that few will likely forget.

Key Points

1. It is likely that there will be a shortage of vaccine doses and that market-based solutions such as auctions will not prove socially acceptable to ration supply.

2. One method of rationing will involve making a list of those who should receive priority such as essential workers and "at risk" populations.

3. It is likely that a lottery mechanism will be used to allocate the majority of doses, but this involves potential inefficiencies even if it is equitable. Allowing a resale market in lottery tickets may allow the best of both worlds by putting people on a level playing field to receive a dose early but allowing them to trade away their place in the line.

4. There may be ways of using priority in future vaccine allocations to provide incentives for positive social behavior in managing the pandemic—such as social distancing and the donation of convalescent plasma.

12

The Future

As in the present crisis, economists did not have a frontline role in World War II and their expertise was primarily applied to management and planning. That allowed some of them room to think about the future. At the time, it was easy to draw a line from the Great Depression to the rise of fascism and, hence, the war. And John Maynard Keynes had seen the problem even earlier in the retribution imposed on Germany following World War I.[1] So it was no surprise that he and his US counterpart, Henry Dexter White, were planning how to do better when the war was over. On April 21, 1944, the Allies came to an agreement to establish new supranational economic institutions to assist in managing the world economy and preventing crises such as the Depression. A preliminary meeting was held in Bretton Woods, New Hampshire, later that year with 730 delegates from 44 countries. It led to establishment of the International Monetary Fund (IMF), an institution that exists to this very day, to allow free conversion of currencies and management of what was then a complex series of fixed exchange rates tied to a fixed price for gold. The goal of the IMF was to provide a means of ensuring that member countries complied and did not adjust their exchange rates wildly for their own short-term motivations. The motives were not retribution but continued cooperation. It was a superior approach.

What will happen once the COVID-19 pandemic has been tamed? It is too early to state definitively what lessons we will have learned or the specifics of how we should respond and react going forward. But there are some general principles likely to be of relevance. For instance, if we look around the world today, the countries that were the closest to previous outbreaks (SARS in 2003 or H1N1 in 2009) enacted clearer plans at an earlier point than others (e.g., Taiwan, Singapore, South Korea, Japan, and China). But while that may have contained COVID-19 outbreaks within their borders, it is plainly apparent that the costs imposed on them because other countries did not have those plans were significant. The global economy is interconnected. If just a few countries manage pandemics appropriately, that does not prevent a large fallout and difficult recovery. In other words, management of the outbreak needs to be global even if its immediate impacts on health are most clearly local.

The issues of international cooperation become more serious when you realize that outbreaks emerge from specific places. In the case of COVID-19, it was in a neighborhood in Wuhan, China. There is insufficient information right now to know whether that outbreak could have been prevented from spreading. But the relevant information was closely held within governments in that area, and, thus, the response and expertise to deal with it had to be similarly confined. The alternative is that there is a *global pandemic response* unit with the expertise and monitoring of health across countries that can come in and dictate appropriate actions to prevent the spread earlier. This creates issues of national sovereignty, cooperation, the bearing of costs, compensation, and myriad other complications. But the social value, globally, from being able to contain an outbreak quickly and close to its source is very high indeed. If the meeting at Bretton Woods could cause countries to cede some control of their international finances to a supranational body, that should at least give us hope that a future global pandemic response institution might be possible.

The question we will want to answer is the following: Knowing what we know now, what institutions would we have liked to see in place with regard to this and future pandemics? My presumption here is that this will likely be a pan-national institution like the IMF with a set of resources to contain future pandemics and ensure an international, harmonized response. The hope is that it would have both public health and economic expertise to do the job properly. Indeed, it may even assume the role of promoting and managing a new Manhattan Project–type innovation offensive against future viruses and disease.

The goal of this final chapter is to highlight the high-level economic challenges that a move in this direction will have to confront. There are political and moral challenges as well, but I will leave those for others to contemplate. My focus here is on how we will determine how much we should spend on managing pandemics proactively going forward.

The Inevitability of Pandemics

Pandemics have some of the mathematical properties of the rice on a chessboard that was discussed in chapter 3 but also some important differences. The main similarity is that it has to start somewhere. The SAR-CoV-2, or novel coronavirus, that causes the disease COVID-19 infected one person initially. That person then housed the virus as it spread throughout their body and then transmitted the virus to others. This can seem like a fluke. However, when you realize there are millions or billions of viruses out there, it was just a matter of time. One of them is going to spread.

The mathematical key here is to realize that we care about how likely one or more of those viruses will become a problem. For any given virus that might be out there, there is a low—perhaps one in a million chance—of it becoming a problem. That sounds comforting until you realize there are a billion such viruses. So, yes, you are rolling a million-sided dice but you are rolling it a billion times and you are hoping never to "win." The probability that one of those rolls will come up the wrong way is so hard to calculate that it is easier to calculate the probability that there won't be a problem (i.e., you'll lose a billion times) and subtracting it from 1:

$$1 - (1 - 1/1,000,000)^{1,000,000,000} = 0.9999999999999999999999999. \ldots$$

This is the probability a virus will become a problem. It isn't 1 but it is very close to 1. If there are only a million viruses, we still get a 63 percent chance that one of them is going to be a problem. The point is that it is inevitable; so inevitable that you would be forgiven if you never wanted to go near another person again.

But we do. And if we do nothing, then, at some point, a pandemic catastrophe will happen. Now it has happened, and the probability that another problematic virus emerges in the future remains close to inevitable.

Prior to COVID-19, our approach to viruses continued to be to accept the inevitable and hope to mitigate and adapt when the time comes. But that strategy relied critically on our ability to accept the mathematics and act quickly. That means we need to know what is going on as early as possible.

In this, I am reminded of a scene from the Cold War movie *Dr. Strangelove*. In it, the Soviets have described a doomsday machine that will be triggered should they be subject to a nuclear attack by the United States. Strangelove himself, modeled loosely on the game theorist and mathematician John von Neumann, remarks on how "essential" it is to deterrence, as no one would attack the Soviet Union if they *knew* it would end up destroying the world and them with it. However, he then exclaims: "but the . . . whole point of the doomsday machine . . . is lost . . . if you keep it a secret! Why didn't you tell the world, eh?" Ultimately, that lack of common knowledge ended up (spoiler alert) destroying the world.

If we are going to act as if viruses are not a concern most of the time, we have to be able to recognize when they do become a concern. Secrets or a lack of knowledge can push us away from sensible behavior. In other words, we need to know and then realize the implications when the first grain of rice is placed on the chessboard. Not having a global monitoring and response institution will continue to leave us all susceptible.

How Much Should Be Paid?

In 2015, Microsoft founder-turned-philanthropist Bill Gates gave a TED talk warning of the costs of a future pandemic and our lack of preparation.[2] The costs of a global flu pandemic were estimated to be in the millions of deaths and a reduction in global wealth of $3 trillion. This was the prediction of a catastrophe. But it was also an indication of what we might be willing to pay to prevent it. The budgets for pandemic preparedness were in the low billions and we know that wasn't enough.

When the benefits are monetary, it is easy to calculate a rate of return on expenditures for preparedness. A reduction in global wealth in the trillions alone suggests that to prevent COVID-19 or another specific pandemic, budgets in the hundreds of billions would still be worthwhile. But my guess is that it will be tough to convince governments to allocate those funds on that basis. Why? Because there are already a number of potential catastrophes that fall into that category of magnitude. Each of those has a different likelihood of happening, but each could happen, impacting on our willingness to pay to prevent any single one. Indeed, when you add up potential global catastrophic risks, one thought you might have is whether it really is worth spending hundreds of billions to avoid one of these things when the others could get us anyway.

That was my thought up until 2015 when a paper appeared that changed my mind. It was written by Ian Martin and Bob Pindyck and was entitled "Averting Catastrophes: The Strange Economics of Scylla and Charybdis."[3] Scylla and Charybdis are a reference to Homer's *The Odyssey*. In that tale, the sailor Odysseus sought to avoid both the sea monster Scylla (a shoal) and the sea monster Charybdis (a whirlpool) but could not avoid both. The choice was made using a cost–benefit analysis: passing by shoal might cause the loss of a few of the crew, but the whirlpool could take the entire ship. The choice for Odysseus was to avoid Charybdis and to pass close to Scylla.

What should we do with regard to the myriad modern catastrophes, especially when we are often faced with decisions that, like Charybdis, could take the entire ship? Not only pandemics but climate change, asteroid strikes, or nuclear war. Martin and Pindyck write:

> Naturally, we would like to avoid all such catastrophes. But even if it were feasible, is that goal advisable? Should we instead avoid some catastrophes and accept the inevitability of others? If so, which ones should we avoid? Unlike Odysseus, we cannot turn to the gods for advice. We must turn instead to economics, the truly dismal science.[4]

Their answer is not to rely on a separate cost–benefit analysis for each one. Nor is their answer to just give up as if there were two whirlpools and no hope. Instead, there is value to picking and choosing which to confront.

To understand this, let's put it in terms of issues that will likely arise: Should we spend money dealing with a future pandemic? Should we spend money dealing with mitigating the climate change disasters that no doubt will come? Both? Or neither? Let's suppose that someone was to argue, What's the point of dealing with pandemics if you believe that we are going to face climate change disasters? The Martin–Pindyck answer is that the case for dealing with pandemics is actually *higher* (not lower) if you are worried about climate change. You should want to deal with it even more intensively than you might have thought.

The intuition is this: if you spend ongoing resources to mitigate pandemics, the fact that you may have to deal with the consequences of a climate emergency (e.g., hurricanes, sea-level rises, extreme heat) means that, in the future, you expect some suffering. That means that you will actually value what you do have *more* and want to spend more to protect it. In other words, if there is harm in your future, you want to spend resources to mitigate another threat because you value what you have more than what you might have had in a disaster-risk-free world. Consider this: if you live in a big house and a fire threatens to potentially raze half of it, you will be willing to spend more to protect the remaining half than you would have spent to protect one of the halves alone.

Once you are expending resources to insure against one catastrophe, the losses you might face if the other one happens are relatively lower. But this raises another question: Which catastrophes should you prioritize? Could it be that concentrating your resources to mitigate a few of them might be better than spreading your resources to deal with them all? You may overstate the returns to tackling one catastrophe if you do, in fact, also deal with another catastrophe. However, an analysis of the costs and benefits of so doing are still informative. For instance, if you assess the mitigation of one catastrophe to have both the highest benefit and lowest cost, you should definitely try to avert that one. Interestingly, Martin and Pindyck's simple calculations suggest that dealing with a global pandemic may fit precisely that bill.

In other words, the message from Martin and Pindyck is not to be fatalistic and give up because you are worried about numerous catastrophes. This analysis gives us strong comfort that, just because we face multiple catastrophes, we should not give up on dealing with some of them. Instead, a cost–benefit analysis should be conducted with an eye to those other risks and what is being done about them. After all, climate change, for instance, is a risk with a different time horizon and profile than pandemics, which are something that could recur quite often. Given that, it is highly unlikely that the case for dealing with one will be undermined if the world chose to deal with the other.

Moreover, in evaluating any catastrophe, assessing things in purely monetary terms is somewhat limited. Pandemics, like some other catastrophes, also have implications with respect to the loss of life. Preventing death is well and truly on the "benefits" side of any set of measures to prevent pandemics. As was discussed in chapter 2, however, being able to really measure these benefits is very difficult.[5]

What this all suggests is that spending hundreds of billions of dollars per year to mitigate substantially the risk of global pandemics is as close to a no-brainer as we are likely to get. That said, prior to COVID-19, we did not engage in that spending. Our experience confirms this error.

What Will Change?

While COVID-19 should not lead to a sizeable change in our willingness to protect ourselves from non-pandemic related catastrophes, there has been considerable speculation as to what it might change in terms of our normal activities. Given the unprecedented nature of the pandemic for nearly a century, thinking about what will change and what might return back to normal can only be speculative. Nonetheless, it seems appropriate to offer a few words of speculation here.

COVID-19 has demonstrated the importance of the internet in our lives. COVID-19 has been manageable in a way that COVID-99 would not have been. We can work and play at home. We can have goods delivered. We can communicate with families and others in distant locations. This suggests that access to the internet will be seen as an essential service going forward, which will have an impact on the broadband policies of many countries. Some of this will be facilitated by workplaces that will rethink the location of their workers. Whether many will continue to work from home is not clear, although some of the more technologically oriented companies like Twitter and Shopify have already announced their intentions to make that mode the default for most employees. What we do not know is how important in-person interactions are for the long-term even if, in the short-term, the productivity impact seemed to be smaller than some might have expected.

More broadly, with respect to online activities, COVID-19 has accelerated trends that might otherwise have taken many years to take hold. This includes opening up more people to video calling and even home delivery of goods than had previously been the case (e.g., prior to 2020, only 14.1% of retail sales globally were online).[6] There are, however, other technological trends that might be accelerated. MIT economist David Autor has called COVID-19 an "automation forcing event."[7] With workers kept away from work, the value of labor-replacing machines has risen for many manufacturing and other businesses. Thus, existing trends toward automation in certain industries may be accelerated.

Finally, there has been discussion that the decades-old trends toward globalization of supply chains may come to an end or be reversed. While there has been recent political pressure toward such moves, some have suggested that businesses and governments looking to make their economies more resilient against supply shocks may renationalize some industries (particularly, in health care). However, this potential conflates disruptions from a pandemic with globalization. Such disruptions could be magnified in future pandemics if governments try to renationalize industries within their borders.[8] For instance, a business on the East Coast of the United States is no less exposed to supply disruptions if it sources key inputs from Asia than from, say, Texas. A pandemic could easily be worse in Texas than in Taiwan and, indeed, COVID-19 was. Even agglomerating an entire supply chain in a single location does not necessarily increase resilience, as it makes it more likely that the entire supply chain will be taken out by a pandemic rather than parts of it that may allow for other sourcing of certain inputs. In other words, whatever the political pressure, there appears to be no strong economic case that a pandemic should change the location of activities in a supply chain.

Future Resolve

Returning to the present, there will come a point in the COVID-19 panic that we will declare victory. At the time of writing, we do not know when that point will be. We do not know the number of deaths the outbreak will cause. We do not know how and whether the economy will bounce back soon after. We do not know whether life will be again regarded as normal. But, right now, for reasons I cannot fully explain, I am confident that there will be a point where we will collectively believe COVID-19 has been conquered.

Then, sadly, the trouble begins. Victory is a dangerous thing. It comes with relief. It comes with exhaustion. It comes with hope that we are done. Therein lies the danger.

World War I was called "the war to end all wars." The victors went back home and were done. For France, this was especially so. They were finished but had also decided to make huge investments to give them a sense of security. They envisaged and then built an incredible series of fortifications along the entire border with Germany. Basically, it was a low-level mountain range with tracks to move troops, 100 miles of tunnels, barracks, and even air conditioning. The Maginot Line would protect France from a direct assault. Half a million troops could be embedded there. No army would try to breach it.

That, of course, was understood by all. If the Germans attacked, they would have to go through the Netherlands and Belgium (or maybe Switzerland). The French plan was to meet the invading force in those countries, which seemed secure. But as with all such things, there were weak links. Belgium decided to stay neutral in World War II. More critically, when the Germans were still preoccupied in the east against Poland, the French army chose not to cross the Maginot Line and preemptively attack. Their strategy had been one of defense. But even Napoleon had said that those who decided to stay within the fortress have already lost. And when the Germans did attack, they managed to slide into France through the Ardennes Forest. It had been believed that the forest was a natural barrier against attack, as it would be slow to traverse. That plan did not account for tanks, which covered the distance in days rather than more than a week.[9] France was cut in two and fell in just over a month. As soon as the invasion had moved to their soil, resolve seemed to evaporate.

The idea that success can breed the seeds of its own destruction is not a new one. In management, the term "disruption" describes the situation where successful businesses cannot adopt new technologies because they continue to do the things that made them successful in the first place.[10] Precisely why it happens and whether it is stupid, complacent,[11] or can be "rationalized" is not material at this point. If and when we are victorious against COVID-19, whatever is driving that phenomenon will likely be present again.[12]

It is also worth noting that, in many respects, COVID-19 was a somewhat "lucky" pandemic. SARS-CoV-2 was far less transmissible than its SARS predecessor or the measles, making it likely that walking outdoors was relatively safe. It did not lead to contaminated food. It appeared to be relatively genetically stable. And it left children (and many others) mostly unaffected. There was no reason for all of those things to have happened. And so, there is no reason to predict that they will be absent in a future pandemic. But there is reason to be worried that we may forget that once we are done with the current crisis.

To build the global institutions needed to mitigate the costs of future pandemics, we will need that resolve. There are signs of hope. The Gates Foundation's move to build manufacturing facilities for seven vaccine candidates, knowing only one or two would be viable, to save months of time is an example. That is what resolve looks like.

More critically, however, we need to take the lessons from understanding the pandemic information problem. Put simply, the experience we had during COVID-19 reinforces the notion that, with early action and a capacity to gather the right information quickly, comes the option of suppressing any viral outbreak rather than allowing the health and economic harm COVID-19 has heaped on many economies. The lesson is that pandemics are manageable. It was done with SARS and MERS, and countries like Vietnam, Mongolia, South Korea, Iceland, and Taiwan did it with COVID-19. The tragedy is their approach was not followed worldwide. How to ensure that it is, is our challenge going forward.

Any victory we have over the next two years needs to come with a warning. The eye cannot be taken off the ball. And if you need any guide from history, remember that we did not get the IMF or the United Nations until we had not one but two world wars.

Notes

Preface

1. *The Onion*, September 26, 2001 (https://local.theonion.com/not-know ing-what-else-to-do-woman-bakes-american-flag-1819566173).

Chapter 1

1. Mike Hume, "Plague, Inc. Removed from China's App Store," *Washington Post*, February 28, 2020.

2. At the beginning of 2020, in terms of popular discussion, the main candidate for human extinction was, and it seems laughable now, artificial intelligence (AI). The robots were coming for our jobs and worse. Indeed, philosopher Nick Bostrom had speculated in his best-selling book, *Superintelligence* (Oxford University Press, 2014), that the way this might occur was through plain old stupidity. One day, a talented engineer would design an AI that would be tasked with making paper clips. That sounds mundane enough, but that design is so good, the AI improves itself and becomes superintelligent. It then applies that intelligence to sucking up all of the world's resources in the mindless pursuit of making more paper clips, killing us all in the process. That both sounded bad and was hard to rule out because we all knew people who made stuff and failed to forecast the consequences. It seemed like a matter of time. Who knew a virus might get us first?

3. One thing that COVID-19 does, which was not an option for players of *Plague Inc.*, is that it impacts different demographics in different ways. While anyone appears to be able to carry the virus and infect others, those who become very sick—requiring hospitalization—tend to be the elderly. That means that in dealing with COVID-19, the costs associated with reduced economic and social activity will disproportionately fall on the young, precisely the group that is less personally impacted. That is a recipe for a virus being able to divide and conquer those who need to mount a response by creating a debate regarding whether that fight was worth it.

4. These calculations are based on http://gabgoh.github.io/COVID/index .html with an $R_0 = 2$ and no interventions.

5. For a clear discussion of endgames, see John Daley, "The Case for Endgame C: Stop Almost Everything, Restart When Coronavirus Is Gone," *The Conversation*, March 20, 2020 (https://theconversation.com/the-case-for -endgame-c-stop-almost-everything-restart-when-coronavirus-is-gone-134 232). In this book, I exposit the case for Endgame C leading to a restart where we can implement Endgame B (test and trace).

6. Brooke Jarvis, "The First Shot: Inside the Covid Vaccine Fast Track," *Wired*, May 13, 2020.

7. The point of herd immunity depends on R_0 (the basic reproduction number that will be discussed in detail in chapter 3). That point is $1 - 1/R_0$, which for an R_0 of 2.5 is 0.6, or 60 percent. These calculations presume that everyone has an equal probability of interacting with anyone else. If that isn't the case then the herd immunity threshold can be lower; see Glenn Ellison, "Implications of Heterogeneous SIR Models for Analyses of COVID-19," *Working Paper*, No. 27373, NBER, June 2020.

8. Carl T. Bergstrom and Natalie Dean, "What the Proponents of 'Natural' Herd Immunity Don't Say," *New York Times*, May 1, 2020.

9. One estimate suggests that no social distancing and minimum protections and testing are required when just one in 36,000 in a population is infected; see Alex Tabarrok and Puja Ahluwalia Ohlhaver, "We Could Stop the Pandemic by July 4 with These Steps," *Washington Post*, May 15, 2020 (https://www.washingtonpost.com/outlook/we-could-stop-the-pandemic -by-july-4-if-the-government-took-these-steps/2020/05/15/9e527370-954f -11ea-9f5e-56d8239bf9ad_story.html).

10. For a very clear articulation of these policy options, see Casey Mulligan, Kevin M. Murphy, and Robert Topel, "Some Basic Economics of COVID-19 Policy," *Chicago Book Review*, April 27, 2020 (https://review .chicagobooth.edu/economics/2020/article/some-basic-economics-covid -19-policy).

11. Economists were thinking about this very quickly. See Richard Baldwin and Beatrice Weder di Mauro (eds.), *Economics in the Time of COVID-19*, March 6, 2020 (https://voxeu.org/content/economics-time-covid-19), and Richard Baldwin and Beatrice Weder di Mauro (eds.), *Mitigating the COVID Economic Crisis: Act Fast and Do Whatever It Takes*, March 18, 2020 (https://voxeu.org/content/mitigating-covid-economic-crisis-act-fast-and -do-whatever-it-takes).

12. Tomas Pueyo calls the containment phrase "the hammer" and the reset phase "the dance." Tomas Pueyo, "Coronavirus: The Hammer and the Dance," *Medium*, March 19, 2020 (https://medium.com/@tomaspueyo /coronavirus-the-hammer-and-the-dance-be9337092b56).

Chapter 2

1. Jack Peat, "President of Ghana Provides Much-Needed Perspective in These Troubling Times," *The London Economic*, March 29, 2020 (https:// www.thelondoneconomic.com/politics/president-of-ghana-provides -much-needed-perspective-in-these-troubling-times/29/03).

2. Eduardo Porter and Jim Tankersley, "Shutdown Spotlights Economic Cost of Saving Lives," *New York Times*, March 24, 2020 (https://www.ny times.com/2020/03/24/business/economy/coronavirus-economy.html).

3. The SIR Model (https://mathworld.wolfram.com/SIRModel.html), which was first introduced in 1927 and models the spread of an infectious disease by calculating who is suspectible (S), infectious (I), and removed (R) over time. For a primer for economics, see Andrew G. Atkeson, "What Will Be the Economic Impact of COVID-19 in the US?," mimeo., UCLA, March 2020 (https://drive.google.com/file/d/1ZWLpUxFZekCTMxCzxZIZ6rWxcX Ah8pUc/view).

4. In *Economics in the Age of COVID-19* (MIT Press, 2020), I cited Sergio Correia, Stephan Luck, and Emil Verner, "Pandemics Depress the Economy, Public Health Interventions Do Not: Evidence from the 1918 Flu,"

March 26, 2020 (https://ssrn.com/abstract=3561560 or http://dx.doi.org/10.2139/ssrn.3561560), as providing support for the notion that dealing with pandemics can improve economic growth prospects. They had studied the 1918 pandemic and found that not engaging in nonpharmaceutical interventions reduced US manufacturing by an estimated 18 percent, making it a large recession indeed. Their results have subsequently been disputed by Andrew Lilley, Matthew Lilley, and Gianluca Rinaldi, "Public Health Interventions and Economic Growth: Revisiting the Spanish Flu Evidence," mimeo., Harvard University, May 2, 2020 (https://almlgr.github.io/paper.pdf), who found no relationship once a longer time series was used. At the time of writing, this debate is still unresolved.

5. This notion has been backed up by some recent economic research on COVID-19 that showed that the pandemic involved a common public health and economic shock across jurisdictions. See Zhixian Lin and Christopher M. Meissner, "Health vs. Wealth? Public Health Policies and the Economy during COVID-19," Working Paper No. 27099, NBER, May 2020.

6. Scott Baker, Nicholas Bloom, Steven Davis, and Stephen Terry, "COVID-Induced Economic Uncertainty and Its Consequences," *VoxEU*, April 13, 2020 (https://voxeu.org/article/covid-induced-economic-uncertainty-and-its-consequences).

7. Susan Athey, Kendall Hoyt, and Michael Kremer, "Everybody Wins from Vaccine Cooperation," *Project Syndicate*, May 14, 2020 (project-syndicate.org/commentary/covid19-vaccine-global-diversified-portfolio-by-susan-athey-et-al-2020-05).

8. Thomas C. Schelling, "The Life You Save May Be Your Own," in *Problems in Public Expenditure Analysis*, ed. Samuel B. Chase, Jr. (Washington, DC: Brookings Institution, 1968), 127–161, and W. Kip Viscusi and Joseph E. Aldy, "The Value of a Statistical Life: A Critical Review of Market Estimates throughout the World," *Journal of Risk and Uncertainty* 27, no. 1 (2003): 5–76.

9. See, for instance, Robert E. Hall, Charles I. Jones, and Peter J. Klenow, "Trading Off Consumption and COVID-19 Deaths," mimeo., Stanford University, June 2020 (http://klenow.com/Consumption_vs_COVID19.pdf).

10. It is worth noting that, with respect to the costs of dealing with COVID-19 (as opposed to the benefits in terms of saved lives), it appears that essential workers are more likely to be women than men (Titan Alon, Mattias Doepke, Jane Olmstead-Rumsey, and Michele Tertilt, "The Impact

of COVID-19 on General Inequality," mimeo., Northwestern University, March 2020, http://faculty.wcas.northwestern.edu/~mdo738/research/ COVID19_Gender_March_2020.pdf, and Simon Mongey and Alex Weinberg, "Characteristics of Workers in Low Work-from-Home and High Personal-Proximity Occupations," mimeo., University of Chicago, March 2020, http://www.simonmongey.com/uploads/6/5/6/6/65665741/mw _covid_occupations_v1.pdf) and younger workers rather than older workers (Andrew Glover, Jonathan Heathcote, Dirk Krueger, and Jose-Victor Rios-Rull, "Health versus Wealth: On the Distributional Effects of Controlling a Pandemic," mimeo., University of Pennsylvania, April 2020 (http:// www.jonathanheathcote.com/healthwealth.pdf).

11. Neil Gandal, Mata Yonas, Michal Feldman, Ady Pauzner, and Avraham Tabbach, "Long-Term Care Facilities as a Risk Factor for Death Due to COVID-19," CEPR Discussion Paper 14844, 2020 (http://cepr.org/active /publications/discussion_papers/dp.php?dpno=14844).

12. Paul Frijters, "The Corona Dilemma," *Club Troppo*, March 21, 2020 (http://clubtroppo.com.au/2020/03/21/the-corona-dilemma/).

13. P. Hanlon, F. Chadwick, A. Shah, et al., "COVID-19—Exploring the Implications of Long-Term Condition Type and Extent of Multimorbidity on Years of Life Lost: A Modelling Study" (version 1; peer review: awaiting peer review). *Wellcome Open Res* 5, no. 75 (2020) (https://doi.org/10 .12688/wellcomeopenres.15849.1).

14. C. J. Ruhm, "Recessions, Healthy no More?," *Journal of Health Economics* 1, no. 42 (2015): 17–28. See also the impact on mental health: Peter H. Huang, "Pandemic Emotions, Public Health, Financial Economics, Law, and Leadership," April 30, 2020, University of Colorado Law Legal Studies Research Paper No. 20-14 (https://ssrn.com/abstract=3575101).

15. Paul Romer, "The Dismal Kingdom," *Foreign Affairs*, March/April 2020 (https://www.foreignaffairs.com/reviews/review-essay/2020-02-11/dismal -kingdom). See also Binyamin Appelbaum, *The Economists' Hour* (Little Brown, 2020), chapter 7.

16. The definition of public health here is somewhat narrow for expository purposes. In reality, actions like social distancing can cause impacts on mental health, in particular, and actions that prioritize treatment of COVID-19 patients may impact on treatments and other health activities that are non-pandemic in nature.

17. Robert J. Barro, "Non-Pharmaceutical Interventions and Mortality in U.S. Cities during the Great Influenza Pandemic, 1918–1919," Working Paper No. 27049, NBER, April 2020.

18. Economist Tyler Cowen, at the beginning of all this, explained the difficulty of forecasting how bad COVID-19 would be. He saw two, quite distinct, camps: "growthers" and "base-raters." Growthers understand exponential growth and the idea that small things can grow into big things quickly. If you see and extrapolate from observations that the number of infected people is doubling in less than a week, you realize that you are a month or so away from a health crisis. Growthers, therefore, tend to be in favor of overreaction at the outset.

The other group, base-raters, which Cowen speculated was initially most people and politicians, understand the mathematics but doubt whether the worst-case scenarios will play out. They tend to look at how things are and wonder if it could really get that bad. It takes a real cognitive effort to become anxious when there are only a few people sick—and, by "few," I mean less than a dozen. Maybe something will interrupt the mathematics. Not every past potential crisis has become a crisis.

See Tyler Cowen, "Bill Gates Is Really Worried about the Coronavirus. Here's Why," *Bloomberg*, March 3, 2020 (https://www.bloomberg.com /opinion/articles/2020-03-03/how-fast-will-the-new-coronavirus-spread -two-sides-of-the-debate).

19. The hollowed-out portion of the PPF is a nonconvexity. This is a direct implication of the SIR model of pandemics. Specifically, if we consider public health as an increasing function of s, the share of susceptible people (as opposed to infected) we have once the pandemic is over, and the economy as an increasing function of R_0 (the basic reproduction number), then it has been calculated that $\text{Log}(s) = R_0(s - 1)$. If you plot this in (R_0, s) space, you will obtain the nonconvex portion in figure 2.2a. See Tiberiu Harko, Francisco Lobo, and M. K. Mak, "Exact Analytical Solutions of the Susceptible–Infected–Recovered (SIR) Epidemic Model and of the SIR Model with Equal Death and Birth Rates," *Applied Mathematics and Computation* 236, no. 1 (2014): 184–194.

20. Before economists jump up and down, it is possible to imagine social utility functions that might cause us to want to be in the "bite." For instance, if economy and health are strict complements, that could easily happen. However, the tendencies that we obtain from a PPF approach

alone tell us that we likely want to prioritize either the economy or public health.

21. Eric Budish, "$R < 1$ as an Economic Constraint: Can We 'Expand the Frontier' in the Fight against Covid-19?," mimeo., University of Chicago Booth School of Business, April 1, 2020 (https://faculty.chicagobooth.edu /eric.budish/research/Budish_expand_the_frontier_covid19.pdf).

22. As explained in chapter 3, this involves targeting a basic reproduction number (R_0) not as low as possible but below 1.

Chapter 3

1. This is a paraphrase of a famous Indian fable; see https://en.wikipedia .org/wiki/Wheat_and_chessboard_problem.

2. If you think that calculation is still somewhat onerous, mathematicians have good news for you. A simple form is this: $T = 2^{64} - 1$.

3. At any point in time, t, Rt is the expected number of people an infectious person is likely to infect at that time. This will vary of the life of the pandemic—rising and then falling. The goal is to get to a point where $Rt < 1$.

4. https://en.wikipedia.org/wiki/Basic_reproduction_number.

5. For an interesting paper on the complexity of R_0, see P. L. Delamater, E. J. Street, T. F. Leslie, Y. T. Yang, and K. H. Jacobsen, "Complexity of the Basic Reproduction Number (R_0)," *Emerging Infectious Diseases* 25, no. 1 (2019): 1–4 (https://doi.org/10.3201/eid2501.171901).

6. Tomas J. Philipson and Richard A. Posner, *Private Choices and Public Health* (Harvard University Press, 1993).

7. See M. Gersovitz and J. S. Hammer, "Infectious Diseases, Public Policy, and the Marriage of Economics and Epidemiology," *World Bank Economic Review* 18, no. 2 (2003): 129–157; M. Gersovitz and J. S. Hammer, "The Economical Control of Infectious Diseases," *The Economic Journal* 114, no. 492 (2004): 1–27; M. Gersovitz, "The Economics of Infection Control," *Annual Review of Resource Economics* 3 (2011): 277–296; Frederick Chen, Jiang Miaohua, Scott Rabidoux, and Stephen Robinson, "Public Avoidance and Epidemics: Insights from an Economic Model," *Journal of Theoretical Biology* 278, no. 1 (2011): 107–119; Eli P. Fenichel, "Economic Considerations for Social Distancing and Behavioral Based Policies during an Epidemic," *Journal of Health Economics* 32, no. 2 (2013): 440–451; Benjamin

R. Morin, Eli P. Fenichel, and Carlos Castillo-Chavez, "SIR Dynamics with Economically Driven Contact Rates," *Natural Resource Modeling* 26, no. 4 (2013): 505–525; Frederick Chen, "A Mathematical Analysis of Public Avoidance Behavior during Epidemics Using Game Theory," *Journal of Theoretical Biology* 302 (2012): 18–28; and Flavio Toxvaerd, "Rational Disinhibition and Externalities in Prevention," *International Economic Review* 60, no. 4 (2019): 1737–1755.

8. Jude Bayham, Nicolai V. Kuminoff, Quentin Gunn, and Eli P. Fenichel, "Measured Voluntary Avoidance Behaviour during the 2009 A/H1N1 Epidemic," *Proceedings of the Royal Society B: Biological Sciences* 282, no. 1818 (2015): 20150814.

9. Michael Springborn, Gerardo Chowell, Matthew MacLachlan, and Eli P. Fenichel, "Accounting for Behavioral Responses during a Flu Epidemic Using Home Television Viewing," *BMC Infectious Diseases* 15, no. 1 (2015): 21.

10. Flavio Toxvaerd, "Equilibrium Social Distancing," mimeo., Cambridge University, 2020. See also M. Eichenbaum, S. Rebelo, and M. Trabandt, "The Macroeonomics of Epidemics," mimeo., Northwestern University, March 2020; Dirk Krueger, Harald Uhlig, and Taojun Xie, "Macroeconomic Dynamics and Reallocation in an Epidemic," Working Paper No. 27047, NBER, April 2020; Zachary Bethune and Anton Korinek, "COVID-19 Infection Externalities: Trading Off Lives vs. Livelihoods," mimeo., University of Virginia, April 2020.

11. Tomas Pueyo, "Coronavirus: The Hammer and the Dance," *Medium*, March 19, 2020, (https://medium.com/@tomaspueyo/coronavirus-the-hammer-and-the-dance-be9337092b56).

12. Maryan Farboodi, Gregor Jarosch, and Robert Shimer, "Internal and External Effects of Social Distancing in a Pandemic," Working Paper No. 2020-47, Becker-Friedman Institute, University of Chiacgo, April 2020.

13. Alexander Chudik, M. Hasham Pesaran, and Alessandrro Rebucci, "Voluntary and Mandatory Social Distancing: Evidence on COVID-19 Exposure Rates from Chinese Provinces and Selected Countries," Working Paper No. 27039, NBER, April 2020; and Austan Goolsbee and Chad Syverson, "Fear, Lockdown, and Diversion: Comparing Drivers of Pandemic Economic Decline 2020," Working Paper, No.27432, NBER, June 2020.

14. Impacting on people's incentives to stay at home would be their comfort levels there. It is arguably the case that in many countries, staying at home is more pleasant than ever due mainly to the internet. However, in this crisis, there is evidence that even within countries such as the United States, there is a wide disparity in home comfort; see Lesley Chiou and Catherine E. Tucker, "Social Distancing, Internet Access and Inequality," April 3, 2020 (https://ssrn.com/abstract=3568255 or http://dx.do.org/10.2139/ssrn.3568255). See also Laura Alfaro, Ester Faia, Nora Lamersdorf, and Farzad Saidi, "Social Interactions in Pandemics: Fear, Altruism, and Reciprocity," Working Paper No. 27134, NBER, May 2020. For a model that takes into account age differences, see Luiz Brotherhood, Philipp Kircher, Cezar Santos, and Michele Tertilt, "An Economic Model of the COVID-19 Epidemic: The Importance of Testing and Age-Specific Policies," Discussion Paper DP14695, CEPR, April 30, 2020.

15. It should be noted that these externalities can be subtle. It is not subtle when people who are infected know it and act in pure self-interest, interacting with others and causing the infection to spread. When a person who is susceptible chooses to avoid interactions, they are protecting themselves but only up to a point. They may, with some probability, become infected and even unknowingly continue to spread the infection. See Lukasz Rachel, "An Analytical Model of Covid-19 Lockdowns," mimeo., London School of Economics, May 2020.

16. This latter externality also arises when people take vaccines. Some people, perhaps those who fear vaccines, decide to opt out of being vaccinated precisely because so many other people are immune.

17. It is possible that if governments do not take action that, say, increases hospital capacity, individuals may decide to try to become infected earlier so that they are not sick when there is a capacity crunch. This fatalism is explored by Callum Jones, Thomas Philippon, and Venky Venkateswaran, "Optimal Mitigation Policies in a Pandemic: Social Distancing and Working from Home," mimeo., New York (https://callumjones.github.io/files/covid.pdf). In a calibrated model for COVID-19, they find that this incentive could well have existed. See also Thomas Kruse and Philipp Strack, "Optimal Control of an Epidemic through Social Distancing," April 20, 2020 (https://papers.ssrn.com/sol3/papers.cfm?abstract_id=3581295).

18. Richard J. Hatchett, Carter E. Mecher, and Marc Lipsitch, "Public Health Interventions and Epidemic Intensity during the 1918 Influenza

Pandemic," *PNAS* 104, no. 18 (May 1, 2007): 7582–7587; first published April 6, 2007 (https://doi.org/10.1073/pnas.0610941104).

19. Matthew Jackson, *The Human Network* (Pantheon Books, 2019), chapter 3. Another factor that slowed the flu in 1918 was having less pollution in one's city. See Karen Clay, Joshua Lewis, and Edson Severnini, "What Explains Cross-City Variation in Mortality during the 1918 Influenza Pandemic? Evidence from 438 U.S. Cities," *Economics and Human Biology* 35 (2019): 42–50.

20. Solomon Hsiang, Daniel Allen, Sebastien Annan-Phan, Kendon Bell, Ian Bolliger, Trinetta Chong, Hannah Druckenmiller, Andrew Hultgren, LunaYue Huang, Emma Krasovich, Peiley Lau, Jaecheol Lee, Esther Rolf, Jeanette Tseng, and Tiffany Wu, "The Effect of Large-Scale Anti-Contagion Policies on the Coronavirus (COVID-19) Pandemic," *medRxiv*, April 2020 (https://doi.org/10.1101/2020.03.22.20040642).

21. The Novel Coronavirus Pneumonia Emergency Response Epidemiology Team, "The Epidemiological Characteristics of an Outbreak of 2019 Novel Coronavirus Diseases (COVID-19)—China, 2020[J]," *China CDC Weekly* 2, no. 8 (2020): 113–122 (http://weekly.chinacdc.cn/en/article/id /e53946e2-c6c4-41e9-9a9b-fea8db1a8f51).

22. For an analysis of how governments should incorporate uncertainty into their response to a novel pandemic, see Michael Barnett, Greg Buchak, and Constantine Yannelis, "Epidemic Responses under Uncertainty," Working Paper No. 27289, NBER, May 2020.

23. The estimates of the total infected had very large ranges. For instance, one estimate for New York in early April 2020 suggested it was possible that as many as 64.5 percent of the population had been infected with the coronavirus and equally possible that only 0.8 percent were infected; see Charles F. Manski and Francesca Molinari, "Estimating the COVID-19 Infection Rate: Anatomy of an Inference Problem," Working Paper No. 27023, NBER, April 2020.

24. James Stock, "Data Gaps and the Policy Response to the Novel Coronavirus," Working Paper No. 26902, NBER, March 2020.

25. https://www.vox.com/2020/4/22/21230301/coronavirus-symptom -asymptomatic-carrier-spread.

26. For an analysis of the consequences of mistiming, see Dylan Morris, Fernando Rossine, Joshua Plotkin, and Simon Levin, "Optimal, Near-

Optimal and Robust Epidemic Control," mimeo., Princeton University, April 3, 2020.

27. Tomas Pueyo, "Coronavirus: The Hammer and the Dance," *Medium*, March 19, 2020 (https://medium.com/@tomaspueyo/coronavirus-the-ham mer-and-the-dance-be9337092b56).

28. Jin Wu, Weiyi Cai, Derek Watkins, and James Glanz, "How the Virus Got Out," *New York Times*, March 22, 2020 (https://www.nytimes.com /interactive/2020/03/22/world/coronavirus-spread.html?referringSource =articleShare).

29. Hannah Beech, Alissa Rubin, Anatoly Kurmanaev, and Ruth Maclean, "The COVID-19 Riddle: Why Does the Virus Wallop Some Places and Spare Others?," *New York Times*, May 3, 2020 (https://www.nytimes.com /2020/05/03/world/asia/coronavirus-spread-where-why.html?referring Source=articleShare).

30. Andrew Atkeson, Karen Kopecky, and Tao Zha, "Estimating and Forecasting Disease Scenarios for COVID-19 with an SIR Model," Working Paper No. 27335 NBER, June 2020.

31. Jim Stock uses the SIR model to show that a critical piece of knowledge is precisely how many in the population are already infected/recovered when you are considering putting social distancing rules in place. If there are few in this category, you want to adopt more extreme social distancing. If there are many, then you can relax, as a good proportion of the population may be immune. The only way to discover the true R_0 at that time is through large sample testing. See J. H. Stock, "Data Gaps and the Policy Response to the Novel Coronavirus," Working Paper 26902, NBER, March 2020.

32. The reader should note that I am using a day for illustration. It may be that information will be expected to arrive in the next week or month.

33. Ben S. Bernanke, "Irreversibility, Uncertainty and Cyclical Investment," *Quarterly Journal of Economics* 98, no. 1 (1983): 85–106.

34. One type of information that might be relevant is what neighboring states and countries are doing, as there is some value to coordinating mitigation efforts; see Zhihan Cui, Geoffrey Heal, and Howard Kunreuther, "Covid-19, Shelter-in-Place Strategies and Tipping," Working Paper No. 27124, NBER, May 2020.

35. This speculation is supported by comparative reports of the decision-making process in Seattle versus New York; see Charles Duhigg, "Seattle's Leaders Let Scientists Take the Lead. New York's Did Not," *The New Yorker*, April 26, 2020 (https://www.newyorker.com/magazine/2020/05/04/seattles -leaders-let-scientists-take-the-lead-new-yorks-did-not).

Chapter 4

1. https://twitter.com/surgeon_general/status/1233725785283932160.

2. https://www.cnn.com/2020/03/30/world/coronavirus-who-masks-rec ommendation-trnd/index.html.

3. Jason Abaluck, Judith A. Chevalier, Nicholas A. Christakis, Howard Paul Forman, Edward H. Kaplan, Albert Ko, and Sten H. Vermund, "The Case for Universal Cloth Mask Adoption and Policies to Increase Supply of Medical Masks for Health Workers," April 1, 2020 (https://ssrn.com /abstract=3567438 or http://dx.doi.org/10.2139/ssrn.3567438).

4. Japanese National Institute of Infectious Diseases, "Field Briefing: Diamond Princess COVID-19 Cases, 20 Feb Update" (https://www.niid.go.jp /niid/en/2019-ncov-e/9417-covid-dp-fe-02.html).

5. A. Davies, K. A. Thompson, K. Giri, G. Kafatos, J. Walker, and A. Bennett, "Testing the Efficacy of Homemade Masks: Would They Protect in an Influenza Pandemic?," *Disaster Medicine and Public Health Preparedness* 7, no. 4 (2013): 413–418; N. M. Ferguson, D. Laydon, G. Nedjati-Gilani, N. Imai, K. Ainslie, M. Baguelin, S. Bhatia, A. Boonyasiri, Z. Cucunubá, G. Cuomo-Dannenburg, and A. Dighe, "Impact of Nonpharmaceutical Interventions (NPIs) to Reduce COVID-19 Mortality and Healthcare Demand," Imperial College, London, 2020 (https://doi.org/10.25561/77482.J).

6. And the evidence is coming in to support this with facemasks improving outcomes by a large amount. See Timo Mitze, Reinhold Kosfeld, Johannes Rode, and Klaus Wälde, "Face Masks Considerably Reduce COVID-19 Cases in Germany: A Synthetic Control Method Approach," Discussion Paper No. 13319, IZA, June 2020.

7. The CDC gave guidance on April 6, 2020, for the creation and use of cloth masks (https://www.cdc.gov/coronavirus/2019-ncov/prevent-getting -sick/diy-cloth-face-coverings.html).

8. I use the word "played" to refer to the fact that experts gave advice to prevent mask adoption by claiming that there were no public health

benefits from using face masks when there was ample evidence that masks would prevent the spread of infections prior to COVID-19. See Davies et al., "Testing the Efficacy"; T. Jefferson, R. Foxlee, C. Del Mar, L. Dooley, E. Ferroni, B. Hewak, A. Prabhala, S. Nair, and A. Rivetti, "Physical Interventions to Interrupt or Reduce the Spread of Respiratory Viruses: Systematic Review," *BMJ* 336, no. 7635 (2008): 77–80; S. Rengasamy, B. Eimer, and R. E. Shaffer, "Simple Respiratory Protection—Evaluation of the Filtration Performance of Cloth Masks and Common Fabric Materials against 20–1000 nm Size Particles," *Annals of Occupational Hygiene*, 54, no. 7 (2010): 789–798; and M. van der Sande, P. Teunis, and R. Sabel, "Professional and Home-made Face Masks Reduce Exposure to Respiratory Infections among the General Population," *PLoS One* 3, no. 7 (2008).

9. As was admitted by Dr. Anthony Fauci in June 2020; Katherine Ross, "Why Weren't We Wearing Masks from the Beginning? Dr. Fauci Explains," *The Street*, June 12, 2020 (https://www.thestreet.com/video/dr -fauci-masks-changing-directive-coronavirus).

10. Some evidence suggests that face masks alone could substantially reduce R_0. See J. Howard, A. Huang, Z. Li, Z. Tufekci, V. Zdimal, H. van der Westhuizen, A. von Delft, A. Price, L. Fridman, L. Tang, V. Tang, G. L. Watson, C. E. Bax, R. Shaikh, F. Questier, D. Hernandez, L. F. Chu, C. M. Ramirez, and A. W. Rimoin, "Face Masks against COVID-19: An Evidence Review," *Preprints 2020*, 2020040203 (doi: 10.20944/preprints 202004.0203.v1).

11. Zeynep Tufekci, Jeremy Howard, and Trisha Greenhalgh, "The Real Reason to Wear a Mask," *The Atlantic*, April 22, 2020 (https://www.the atlantic.com/health/archive/2020/04/dont-wear-mask-yourself/610336).

12. https://onemocneni-aktualne.mzcr.cz/covid-19.

13. Zeynep Tufekci, "Why Telling People They Don't Need Masks Backfired," *New York Times*, March 17, 2020 (https://www.nytimes.com/2020 /03/17/opinion/coronavirus-face-masks.html).

14. This is what Noah Smith suggested when he advocated the use of apps that inform people of where there are stocks of essential goods. Such apps had been deployed to inform consumers of where face masks were for sale in Taiwan. See Noah Smith, "How to Limit Hoarding and Keep America's Hands Clean," *Bloomberg Opinion*, March 19, 2020 (https://www .bloomberg.com/opinion/articles/2020-03-19/rationing-and-tech-can -limit-covid-19-soap-toilet-paper-hoarding).

15. Jemima Kelly, "Is It Acceptable for the Government to Be Dishonest at a Time like This?," *Financial Times*, April 30, 2020 (https://ftalphaville .ft.com/2020/04/30/1588242892000/Is-it-acceptable-for-government-to -be-dishonest-at-a-time-like-this--/).

16. For a recent review of studies of effective government policy making in the face of viral outbreaks, see Imran Rasul, "The Economics of Viral Outbreaks," *AEA Papers and Proceedings* 111 (2020): 265–268.

17. This is an example of Bayesian persuasion (see Emir Kamenica and Matthew Gentzkow, "Bayesian Persuasion," *American Economic Review* 101, no. 6 (2011): 2590–2615). As an example, suppose that there is no pandemic, a mild pandemic, or a serious pandemic, and each of these three events occurs with probability 1/3. Suppose that people get 1/2 if they don't wear a mask, –1 if they wear a mask and there is no pandemic, 1 if they wear a mask during a mild pandemic, and 2 during a serious one. In this case, if they had no information, they would get (2/3 + 1/3 – 1/3) = 2/3 from wearing a mask and 1/2 from not and so would choose to wear one. If they are told the full truth—that is, that there is a pandemic when there is either a mild or serious one—people would wear a mask because they would receive 3/2 rather than 1/2. But what if public health officials did not want people to have masks if there is a mild pandemic (or perhaps a shortage of masks) but did want people to have masks if it is serious? No information or telling the full truth won't get that outcome. They could tell people there is no pandemic if it is mild. People would understand that they were downplaying the pandemic truth but, on net, would still expect to receive 0 from wearing a mask and so would choose not to do so. By contrast, if people got 2 if they did not wear a mask, then even if it is a mild pandemic, you might want to tell them there is a pandemic (at least some of the time), so you could nudge them over the edge into mask wearing. In other words, if the default is to wear masks, you try to be clear when you really need them to wear masks, and if the default is to not wear masks, you try to be clear when you don't need them to wear masks.

18. Thinking about the delivery of information has been a theme in health management. See, for instance, Nikolaus Schweizer and Nora Szech, "Optimal Revelation of Life-Changing Information," *Management Science* 64, no. 11 (2018): 5250–5262.

19. Tufekci, "Why Telling People They Don't Need Masks Backfired."

20. For a full analysis of authority versus persuasion, see Eric Van den Steen, "Authority versus Persuasion," *American Economic Review* 99, no. 2 (2009): 448–453.

21. Emily Oster, "The 'Just Stay Home' Message Will Backfire," *The Atlantic*, May 14, 2020 (https://www.theatlantic.com/ideas/archive/2020/05/just-stay-home-message-will-backfire/611623).

22. There is evidence that the form of the communication matters. One paper (Guglielmo Briscese, Nicola Lacetera, Mario Macis, and Mirco Tonin, "Compliance with COVID-19 Social-Distancing Measures in Italy: The Role of Expectations and Duration," Working Paper No. w26916, NBER, 2020) found in a survey conducted during COVID-19 in Italy that pessimistic forecasts were easier to walk back from than optimistic ones in establishing future community trust.

23. We should recognize, however, that when it comes to health risks, people can often be poor judges of their own risk in the face of uncertainty. Information provision can counter that. See Emily Oster, Ira Shoulson, and E. Dorsey, "Optimal Expectations and Limited Medical Testing: Evidence from Huntington Disease," *American Economic Review* 103, no. 2 (2013): 804–830.

24. For a discussion, see John Zarocostas, "How to Fight an Infodemic," *The Lancet* 395 (February 29, 2002): 676.

25. See Matthew Jackson, *The Human Network* (Pantheon Books, 2019), 177–179, for a discussion.

26. Leonardo Bursztyn, Aakaash Rao, Christopher Roth, and David Tanagizawa-Drott, "Misinformation during a Pandemic," mimeo., University of Chicago, April 19, 2020 (https://www.dropbox.com/s/7nl9998 zuwdk81i/Misinformation_During_a_Pandemic.pdf?dl=1). See also Andrey Simonov, Szymon K. Sacher, Jean-Pierre H. Dubé, and Shirsho Biswas, "The Persuasive Effect of Fox News: Non-Compliance with Social Distancing during the Covid-19 Pandemic," Working Paper No. 27237, NBER, May 2020.

27. Hunt Allcott, Levi Boxell, Jacob Conway, Matthew Gentzkow, Michael Thaler, and David Yang, "Polarization and Public Health: Partisan Differences in Social Distancing during COVID-19," Working Paper, Stanford University, 2020; and John Manuel Barrios and Yael V. Hochberg, "Risk Perception through the Lens of Politics in the Time of the COVID-19

Pandemic," University of Chicago, Becker Friedman Institute for Economics Working Paper, 2020 (2020-32).

28. There are many examples of this happening with COVID-19; see Charlie Warzel, "What We Pretend to Know about the Coronavirus Could Kill Us," *New York Times*, April 3, 2020 (https://www.nytimes.com/2020/04/03/opinion/sunday/coronavirus-fake-news.html).

29. Abhijit V. Banerjee, "The Economics of Rumours," *The Review of Economic Studies* 60, no. 2 (1993): 309–327.

30. This was also a lesson from the 1918 pandemic; see J. Barry, "Pandemics: Avoiding the Mistakes of 1918," *Nature* 459 (2009): 324–325 (https://doi.org/10.1038/459324a). It was noted that the US government's response was similar to its response to war information: to quell fear and worry. In that case, downplaying the risks potentially assisted in the spread of the virus.

Chapter 5

1. John Maynard Keynes, "How to Pay for the War," in *Essays in Persuasion* (Palgrave Macmillan, 2010), 367–439.

2. Indeed, Bill Janeway argued that the level of governmental competence was not the same as it was in World War II to achieve these outcomes (https://www.project-syndicate.org/commentary/covid19-is-not-wartime-mobilization-by-william-janeway-2020-04).

3. *Micromotives and Macrobehavior* (Norton, 1978), 20.

4. Patrick Bolton and Joseph Farrell, "Decentralization, Duplication, and Delay," *Journal of Political Economy* 98, no. 4 (1990): 803–826.

5. Some will note that perhaps market or mechanism design could give us the best of both worlds. Bolton and Farrell deal with that, but some of the baseline trade-offs remain. Also, design takes time and must be matched to every crisis, so it does not seem feasible.

6. Economists have demonstrated that, in the absence of a change in healthcare capacity or vaccine, the notion of "flattening the curve" is not the best policy. This is because, at its peak, the flattened curve just meets healthcare capacity, and so, by definition, most of the time capacity is underutilized. They show that it would be better to let the infections grow

until they are likely to hit the capacity limit and then engage in a strong lockdown and then gradual easing to "fill the box" and utilize capacity over a longer time period. See Laurent Miclo, Daniel Spiro, and Jörgen Weibull, "Optimal Epidemic Suppression under an ICU Constraint," May 5, 2020 (https://arxiv.org/abs/2005.01327).

7. Bolton and Farrell, "Decentralization, Duplication, and Delay."

8. Daniel M. Horn, "How America Can Avoid Italy's Ventilator Crisis," *New York Times*, March 22, 2020 (https://www.nytimes.com/2020/03/22/opinion/health/ventilator-shortage-coronavirus-solution.html?smtyp=cur&smid=tw-nytopinion).

9. Susan Adams, "The Economics of Panic Buying," *Forbes*, March 5, 2020 (https://www.forbes.com/sites/susanadams/2020/03/05/the-economics-of-panic-buying/#647d46e85e27). Indeed, some of us thought that people could certainly economize on the toilet paper they had or switch to alternatives like bidets.

10. That said, they are at home more so there may be a shift in the allocation of "activity." Nonetheless, this is analogous to the types of shortages that arose during the Soviet Union based on consumer hoarding of products they expected to be off the shelves quickly, like soap. See Martin L. Weitzman, "Price Distortion and Shortage Deformation, or What Happened to the Soap?," *American Economic Review* (June 1, 1991): 401–414.

11. Jack Nicas, "He Has 17,700 Bottles of Hand Sanitizer and Nowhere to Sell Them," *New York Times*, March 14, 2020 (https://www.nytimes.com/2020/03/14/technology/coronavirus-purell-wipes-amazon-sellers.html).

12. John K. Galbraith, "The Disequilibrium System," *American Economic Review* 37, no. 3 (1947): 298, note 16.

13. Piotr Dworczak, Scott Duke Kominers, and Mohammad Akbarpour, "Redistribution through Markets," December 24, 2019, Becker Friedman Institute for Research in Economics Working Paper No. 2018-16 (https://ssrn.com/abstract=3143887).

14. Scott Duke Kominers, "Keep Sanitizer Out of the Invisible Hand," *Bloomberg*, March 16, 2020 (https://www.bloomberg.com/opinion/articles/2020-03-16/coronavirus-emergency-why-price-gouging-for-sanitizer-is-wrong).

15. David Katz, "Is Our Fight against Coronavirus Worse than the Disease?," *New York Times*, March 20, 2020 (https://www.nytimes.com/2020/03/20/opinion/coronavirus-pandemic-social-distancing.html).

16. Daron Acemoglu, Victor Chernozhukov, Iván Werning, and Michael D. Whinston, "A Multi-Risk SIR Model with Optimally Targeted Lockdown," Working Paper No. 27102, NBER, May 2020. See also V. V. Chari, Rishabh Kirplani, and Christopher Phelan, "The Hammer and the Scalpel: On the Economics of Discriminate versus Targeted Isolation Policies during Pandemics," mimeo., University of Minnesota, May 2020.

17. Alex Tabarrok, "The Internal Contradictions of Segregating the Elderly," *Marginal Revolution*, March 22, 2020 (https://marginalrevolution.com/marginalrevolution/2020/03/the-internal-contradictions-of-segregating-the-elderly.html). See also Megan McArdle, "Here's Why It Won't Work to Just Isolate the Vulnerable," *Washington Post*, April 3, 2020 (https://www.washingtonpost.com/opinions/2020/04/03/heres-why-it-wont-work-just-isolate-elderly-vulnerable/).

18. There are challenges in enforcing them. In Spain, dog walking was permitted and so markets sprang up to match dog owners with others who needed to get about. See "Walking the Dog: A Get-Out-of-Jail Card in Lockdown Spain," *France24*, March 19, 2020 (https://www.france24.com/en/20200319-walking-the-dog-a-get-out-of-jail-card-in-lockdown-spain?fbclid=IwAR2kdovFMNRMwz37e_A-UF_C6E_O6sDthfqxem1lE4Wiebneh0zj5rfy8MU). It goes without saying that dogs received great benefits from widespread social distancing.

19. The island of Hokkaido in Japan had a successful suppression initially so opened their economy quickly only to find that this attracted infected people from elsewhere in Japan, forcing a second and longer lockdown. Abigail Leonard, "This Japanese Island Lifted Its Coronavirus Lockdown Too Soon and Became a Warning to the World," *Time*, April 24, 2020 (https://time.com/5826918/hokkaido-coronavirus-lockdown).

Chapter 6

1. One of the earliest descriptions and prescriptions for the economy came from Steven Hamilton and Stan Veuger, "A Recession Is a Public Health Necessity. Here's How to Make It Short and Sharp," *The Bulwark*, March 14, 2020 (https://thebulwark.com/a-recession-is-a-public-health-necessity-heres-how-to-make-it-short-and-sharp). They wrote: "The key

thing to grasp is that this will be no normal recession. Economics text-books don't cover how to deal with the fallout from a global pandemic."

2. The HIV/AIDS crisis was of a similar magnitude in terms of deaths but was spread out for many more years.

3. Robert J. Barro, Jose F. Ursua, and Joanna Weng, "The Coronavirus and the Great Influenza Epidemic: Lessons from the 'Spanish Flu' for the Coronavirus' Potential Effects on Mortality and Economic Activity," AEI Economics Working Paper 2020-02, March 2020.

4. In particular, it has grave distributional consequences, hitting disadvantaged groups harder and, in this case, likely to be felt more by women than men. Usually, recessions cause more men to lose their jobs than women (see Hilary Hoynes, Douglas L. Miller, and Jessamyn Schaller, "Who Suffers during Recessions?," *Journal of Economic Perspectives* 26, no. 3 (2012): 27–48), but this time there is reason to believe that the impact may be larger on women especially given the impact of a lack of childcare and schooling. See Titan Alon, Mathias Doepke, Jane Olmstead-Rumsey, and Michele Tertilt, "The Impact of COVID-19 on Gender Inequality," *Covid Economics* 4 (April 2020): 62–85. Finally, some have argued that these distributional concerns should motivate policies that favor a weaker shutdown of economic activity; see Andrew Glover, Jonathan Heathcote, Dirk Krueger, and Jose-Victor Rios-Rull, "Health versus Wealth: On the Distributional Effects of Controlling a Pandemic," Working Paper No. 27046, NBER, April 2020.

5. https://twitter.com/Austan_Goolsbee/status/1239649835969646592 ?s=20.

6. Perhaps the most complete articulation to date regarding how this recession will differ from normal ones and what this means for policy has been provided by Veronica Guerrieri, Guido Lorenzoni, Ludwig Straub, and Ivan Werning, "Macroeconomic Implications of COVID-19: Can Negative Supply Shocks Cause Demand Shortages?," mimeo., MIT, April 2020 (https://economics.mit.edu/files/19351).

7. Scott Ellison quoted by Tyler Cowen, "Stopping Time: An Approach to Pandemics?," *Marginal Revolution*, March 19, 2020 (https://marginalrevo lution.com/marginalrevolution/2020/03/stopping-time-an-approach-to -pandemics.html).

8. Different metaphors have been used to describe this type of policy direction. While I have chosen to use "pause" here, others have used

hibernation, medically induced coma (and thereby requiring life support), and a freeze. If I had could have my way, I would have gone with "frozen in carbonite."

9. https://www.cloverfoodlab.com/2020/03/17/psa-call-for-help-please-if -you-run-a-tech-services-company-offer-your-restaurant-clients-3-months -credit-asap.

10. What this pause notion does not quite capture is what to do about potential disruption and restarting of complicated supply chains. See Matthew Elliott, Benjamin Golub, and Matthew V. Leduc, "Supply Network Formation and Fragility," mimeo., Harvard University, April 3, 2020 (http://bengolub.net/papers/SNFF.pdf).

11. https://www.antievictionmap.com/covid.

12. Steven Erlanger, "Macron Declares France 'at War' with Virus, as EU Proposes 30 Day Travel Ban," *New York Times*, March 16, 2020 (https:// www.nytimes.com/2020/03/16/world/europe/coronavirus-france-macron -travel-ban.html).

13. Derek Thompson, "Denmark's Idea Could Help the World Avoid a Great Depression," *The Atlantic*, March 21, 2020 (https://www.theatlantic .com/ideas/archive/2020/03/denmark-freezing-its-economy-should-us /608533/?utm_source=nextdraft&utm_medium=email).

14. Emmanuel Saez and Gabriel Zucman, "The Crisis Calls for Massive Government Intervention: Here's How to Do It," *The Guardian*, March 17, 2020 (https://www.theguardian.com/commentisfree/2020/mar/17/govern ments-crisis-coronavirus-business).

15. The idea of making adjustments after the fact rather than before gained some traction during the crisis. This was earlier articulated by Claudia Sahm, "Direct Stimulus Payments to Individuals," in Heather Boushey, Ryan Nunn, and Jay Shambaugh (eds.), *Recession Ready: Fiscal Policies to Stabilize the U.S. Economy* (2019), and then by Greg Mankiw at http://greg mankiw.blogspot.com/2020/03/a-proposal-for-social-insurance-during .html.

16. Sendhil Mullainathan, "We All Need Small Businesses. Don't Let Them Die," *New York Times*, March 19, 2020 (https://www.nytimes.com /2020/03/19/business/small-businesses-coronavirus-help.html).

17. Peter Ganong and Pascal Noel, "Liquidity vs. Wealth in Household Debt Obligations: Evidence from Housing Policy in the Great Recession," mimeo., University of Chicago, 2020.

18. Joshua Gans and Stephen King, "The Housing Lifeline: A Policy for Short-Run Housing Affordability," *Agenda* 11, no. 2 (2004). See also comments by Bruce Chapman at https://www.anu.edu.au/news/all-news/hecs-style-loans-can-help-beat-the-coronavirus-cash-crisis.

19. One might ask: Could this have all been achieved by having pandemic insurance—that is, a way for people and businesses to pay a premium for a payout should a pandemic arise? The issue there is that a pandemic is a systemic shock and there are few people who see an upside. That is important, as otherwise a pandemic could send the insurer to bankruptcy. One group did identify a potential counterparty—pension funds. For them, a pandemic was a potential (albeit morbid) windfall as it reduced the life expectancy of recipients. This is an emerging area, and it is reasonable to expect that it will gain more interest post-pandemic. See Evan Ratliff, "This Is Nathan Wolfe. We Should Have Listened to Him," *Wired*, July/August 2020.

20. For instance, some of the job losses may be concentrated in parts of the economy where it can take many years to find stable jobs; see Victoria Gregory, Guido Menzio, and David G. Wiczer, "Pandemic Recession: L or V-Shaped?," Working Paper No. 27105, NBER, May 2020.

Chapter 7

1. Joseph E. Aldy and W. Kip Viscusi, "Risk Regulation Lessons from Mad Cows," *Foundations and Trends in Microeconomics* 8, no. 4 (2013): 231–313.

2. Details of this case are drawn from Aldy and Viscusi, "Risk Regulation Lessions."

3. Bryan Caplan, *The Case against Education: Why the Education System Is a Waste of Time and Money* (Princeton University Press, 2018).

4. See Paul Romer and Alan M. Garber, "Will Our Economy Die from Coronavirus?," *New York Times*, March 23, 2020 (https://www.nytimes.com/2020/03/23/opinion/coronavirus-depression.html?searchResultPosition =1); and Alex Tabarrok, "A Solution if We Act," *Marginal Revolution*, March 30, 2020 (https://marginalrevolution.com/marginalrevolution/2020/03/a-solution-if-we-act.html). However, the genesis of this idea was a post

by Tomas Pueyo, "Coronavirus: The Hammer and the Dance," *Medium*, March 14, 2020 (https://medium.com/@tomaspueyo/coronavirus-the-ham mer-and-the-dance-be9337092b56). His hammer reflected the contain- ment phase I have discussed, while the dance was testing and tracing as part of the reset phase. Some formal modeling of the economic value of testing is contained in Facundo Piguillem and Liyan Shi, "The Optimal COVID-19 Quarantine and Testing Policies," Working Paper, 20/04, EIEF, March 2020 (http://www.eief.it/eief/images/WP_20.04.pdf).

5. Gretchen Vogel, "New Blood Tests for Antibodies Could Show True Scale of Coronavirus Pandemic," *Science*, March 19, 2020 (https://www .sciencemag.org/news/2020/03/new-blood-tests-antibodies-could-show -true-scale-coronavirus-pandemic).

6. For more details of the two types of test, see M. Dewatripont, M. Gold- man, E. Muraille, and J.-P. Platteau, "Rapidly Identifying Workers Who Are Immune to COVID-19 and Virus-Free Is a Priority for Restarting the Economy," VoxEU.org, March 23, 2020 (https://voxeu.org/article/rapidly -identifying-workers-who-are-immune-covid-19-and-virus-free-priority -restarting-economy).

7. Donato Paolo Mancini and Clive Cookson, "Aggressive Testing Helps Italian Town Cut New Coronavirus Cases to Zero," *Financial Times*, March 17, 2020 (https://www.ft.com/content/0dba7ea8-6713-11ea-800d -da70cff6e4d3).

8. Toward the end of March 2020, medical practitioners began observing that many COVID-19 cases were accompanied by a loss of sense of taste and/or smell. If this were the case, then it would provide a solid symptom- atic way of identifying those who have the virus by putting them in close proximity to a dog or teenager. For more, see Michael Lewis, "A Corona- virus Fix That Passes the Smell Test," *Bloomberg*, April 1, 2020 (https:// www.bloomberg.com/opinion/articles/2020-04-01/tracking-coronavirus -by-smell-test-is-risk-manager-s-project-now), and Joshua Gans, "Smell Test Now," *Medium*, April 1, 2020 (https://medium.com/@joshgans/smell-test -now-2bf533d8b955). Using Google trends information, Seth Stephens- Davidowitz also conjectured eye pain may be a symptom; see "Google Searches Can Help Us Find Emerging Covid-19 Outbreaks," *New York Times*, April 5, 2020 (https://www.nytimes.com/2020/04/05/opinion /coronavirus-google-searches.html). There may also be other ways symp- toms can be measured at an individual level and then aggregated up to

see where outbreaks may be emerging; see Lauren Goode, "Can a Wearable Detect Covid-19 before Symptoms Appear?," *Wired*, April 14, 2020 (https://www.wired.com/story/wearable-covid-19-symptoms-research).

9. If there is a flu test, then the information from the test can be used to potentially raise the relevance of co-symptoms if the flu test turns out to be negative for an individual.

10. There were estimates that for COVID-19, if 70 percent of contacts from someone who tested positive could be traced, this would be sufficient to reduce R_0 below one and end the pandemic. See John Hellewell, Sam Abbott, Amy Gimma, et al., "Feasibility of Controlling COVID-19 Outbreaks by Isolation of Cases and Contacts," *The Lancet*, February 28, 2020 (https://doi.org/10.1016/S2214-109X(20)30074-7).

11. Ofir Reich, Guy Shalev, and Tom Kalvari, "Modeling COVID-19 on a Network: Super-Spreaders, Testing and Containment," mimeo., Tel Aviv University, April 28, 2020.

12. Digital technologies are being deployed to assist with contact tracing through community reporting of symptoms and cases and also the use of mobile phone tracking (https://www.foreignaffairs.com/articles/asia/2020-03-20/how-civic-technology-can-help-stop-pandemic). In April 2020, Apple and Google announced plans to develop contact tracing capabilities on both the iOS and Android mobile operating systems. Of course, these raise issues of surveillance and privacy that will not be easily resolved. That said, some innovators have been able to develop methods of contact tracing that appear to be able to protect privacy of those being traced. (An example of this is the Safepaths app developed by a team at MIT: http://safepaths.mit.edu.) For a broader discussion of these methods, see Vi Hart et al., "Outpacing the Virus: Digital Response to Containing the Spread of COVID-19 while Mitigating Privacy Risks," COVID-19 Rapid Response Impact Initiative, White Paper No. 5, Edmond J. Safra Center for Ethics, Harvard University, April 3, 2020 (https://ethics.harvard.edu/files/center-for-ethics/files/white_paper_5_outpacing_the_virus_final.pdf), and, from Nicky Case, see https://ncase.me/contact-tracing/?v=2 for a graphic description of how we may be able to have our cake and eat it too.

13. See David Berger, Kyle Herkenhoff, and Simon Mongey, "An SEIR Infectious Disease Model with Testing and Conditional Quarantine," mimeo., Duke University, March 24, 2020 (http://www.simonmongey.com/uploads/6/5/6/6/65665741/bhm_corona_v4.pdf).

14. Paul Romer laid out a plan for this type of approach, *A Roadmap to Responsibly Reopen America* (https://roadmap.paulromer.net), April 2020. It calls for widespread weekly or biweekly testing of the entire population and does not use contact tracing.

15. Sam Peltzman, "The Effects of Automobile Safety Regulation," *Journal of Political Economy* 83, no. 4 (1975): 677–725.

16. Subsequent studies reinforced these findings. See Björn Lindgren and Charles Stuart, "The Effects of Traffic Safety Regulation in Sweden," *Journal of Political Economy* 88, no. 2 (1980): 412–427; Robert W. Crandall and John D. Graham, "Automobile Safety Regulation and Offsetting Behavior: Some New Empirical Estimates," *The American Economic Review* 74, no. 2 (1984): 328–331; and Theodore E. Keeler, "Highway Safety, Economic Behavior, and Driving Environment," *The American Economic Review* 84, no. 3 (1994): 684–693.

17. A recent paper showed theoretically that such rebounds associated with testing could lead to a higher rate of infection. See Daron Acemoglu, Ali Makhdoumi, Azarakhsh Malekian, and Asuman Ozdaglar, "Testing, Voluntary Social Distancing, and the Spread of an Infection," Working Paper No.27483, NBER, July 2020.

18. Kathryn Olivarius, "Immunity, Capital and Power in Antebellum New Orleans," *American Historical Review* 124, no. 2 (April 2019): 425.

19. At least if you were white. Olivarius found that for blacks, by being acclimated, they became only more valuable slaves.

20. Germany reportedly will introduce certification for those who have recovered from COVID-19 (https://www.telegraph.co.uk/news/2020/03/29 /germany-will-issue-coronavirus-antibody-certificates-allow-quarantined). Dare I say it that this might be time for the blockchain! See Christian Catalini and Joshua Gans, "Some Simple Economics of the Blockchain," *Communications of the ACM*, forthcoming. Others have suggested that some form of group testing could result in higher speed and lower testing costs. See Olivier Gossner, "Group Testing against COVID-19," mimeo., CREST, March 29, 2020 (http://gossner.me/wp-content/uploads/2020/03 /group-testing20202328.pdf), and Christian Gollier, "Optimal Group Testing to Exit the Cover Confinement," mimeo., Toulouse School of Economics, March 2020 (https://www.tse-fr.eu/sites/default/files/TSE/documents /doc/by/gollier/group_testing.pdf). This type of group testing was being carried out in Nebraska, but, at least in the United States, such methods

were not generally permissible under health regulations; see Jordan Ellenberg, "Five People. One Test, This Is How You Get There," *New York Times*, May 7, 2020 (https://www.nytimes.com/2020/05/07/opinion/coronavirus-group-testing.html). Recent research has suggested that group testing combined with machine learning could actually become more efficient over time and dramatically reduce the ongoing costs of widespread testing; see Ned Augenblick, Jonathan T. Kolstad, Ziad Obermeyer, and Ao Wang, "Group Testing in a Pandemic: The Role of Frequent Testing, Correlated Risk, and Machine Learning," Working Paper, No. 27457, NBER, July 2020.

21. Daniel Jacob Hemel and Anup Malani, "Immunity Passports and Moral Hazard," May 8, 2020 (https://ssrn.com/abstract=3596569).

22. For a full discussion, see Charles F. Manski, "Bounding the Predictive Values of COVID-19 Antibody Tests," Working Paper, No. 27226, NBER, May 2020. See also Jeffrey Ely, Andrea Galeotti and Jakub Steiner, "Optimal Test Allocation," mimeo., Northwestern University, May 2020 (http://home.cerge-ei.cz/steiner/allocation.pdf).

23. How much of the population would have to have been infected for HAD tests to work? Suppose that the false positive rate is p and the false negative rate is n. If a share x of the population have been infected, then the probability that a person who passes a HAD test is immune is $(1 - n)x/((1 - n)x + p(1 - x))$. Thus, suppose that we are happy to confer immunity if you have a 9/10 chance of being immune, then we want $(1 - n)x/((1 - n)x + p(1 - x)) > 0.9$ or $x > 0.9p/(0.1(1 - n) + 0.9p)$. If $p = n = 0.05$, this implies $x > 0.32$, or 32 percent.

24. In the case of COVID-19, the main factors are whether there is RNA material on the swab (or enough to be detected), whether it contains the RNA sequence matching COVID-19, and whether there no other PCR failures.

25. David Louie, "COVID-19 Testing Is Important but Has 10 to 15% Rate of Producing False, Negative Results, Pathologist Says," *ABC7 News*, March 26, 2020 (https://abc7news.com/6053940).

26. https://paulromer.net/covid-sim-part3.

27. https://paulromer.net/covid-sim-part2.

28. Biochemists Jussi Taipale and Sten Linnarsson (https://medium.com/@sten.linnarsson/to-stop-covid-19-test-everyone-373fd80eb03b) point out that we can potentially get away with testing fewer people in the

population if we want to get the basic reproduction number below 1. If we identify someone as positive and quarantine them, suppose that instead of R_0 the basic reproduction number for quarantined people is R_q ($< R_0$). If we test a proportion of the population, c, and if our test has a true positive rate of p, then the average basic reproduction number is $cpR_q + (1 - cp)R_0$. We want this to be less than 1, so $cp > (R_0 - 1)/(R_0 - R_q)$. If $R_0 = 2.4$ and $R_q = 0.3$, then we need $cp > 2/3$. Interestingly, for an accurate test, the higher the prevalence of the virus in the population, the *lower* is the amount of testing you need. See also Berger et al., "An SEIR Infectious Disease Model."

29. See Matthew Cleevely, Daniel Susskind, David Vines, Louis Vines, and Sam Wills, "A Workable Strategy for Covid-19 Testing: Stratified Period Testing Rather than Universal Random Testing," mimeo., Oxford University, April 15, 2020 (https://static1.squarespace.com/static/57d002e0 1b631bc215df193b/t/5e96e6ad445bca269b0671c0/1586947760671/strati fied_periodic_testing_2_p.pdf).

30. Because the coronavirus tended to mutate every two transmissions or so, genetic tracing offers another way to analyze the spread of COVID-19. This additional information allowed researchers in San Francisco to determine that two cases of COVID-19 at a fish packing plant came from separate sources and so avoided the need to shut the plant down; see Michael Lewis, "The New Weapon in the COVID-19 War," *Bloomberg*, June 22, 2020 (https://www.bloomberg.com/graphics/2020-opinion-chan-zuckerberg -biohub-covid-tracing).

31. Tim Harford, "The Statistical Detective Work Required to Ease Lockdown," *Financial Times*, May 8, 2020.

32. That share is $(R_0 - 1)/R_0$. So, if the R_0 for COVID-19 is greater than 2, at least half of the population will be infected at any given time. See Chryssi Giannitsarou, Stephen Kissler and Flavio Toxvaerd, "Waning Immunity and the Second Wave: Some Projections for SARS-CoV-2," mimeo., Cambridge University, 2 June 2020.

33. For a discussion, see Robert Rowthorn and Flavio Toxvaerd, "The Optimal Control of Infectious Diseases via Prevention and Treatment," mimeo., Cambridge University, 2017.

34. Gregory Barber, "What If Covid-19 Returns Every Year, like the Common Cold?," *Wired*, April 15, 2020 (https://www.wired.com/story /what-if-covid-19-returns-every-year-like-the-common-cold).

35. Park Si-soo, "South Korea Confirms 111 Cases of Coronavirus Rein-fection," *The Korea Times*, April 12, 2020 (https://www.koreatimes.co.kr/www/nation/2020/04/119_287752.html). There were also similar cases reported in Shenzhen and Wuhan China.

36. C. J. Wang, C. Y. Ng, and R. H. Brook, "Response to COVID-19 in Taiwan: Big Data Analytics, New Technology, and Proactive Testing," *JAMA*, published online March 3, 2020 (doi:10.1001/jama.2020.3151).

37. See Gary Pisano, Raffaella Sadun, and Michele Zanini, "Lessons from Italy's Response to the Coronavirus," *Harvard Business Review* online, March 27, 2020 (https://hbr.org/2020/03/lessons-from-italys-response-to-coronavirus).

Chapter 8

1. "Love in the Time of HIV: Testing as a Signal of Risk," mimeo., University of Toronto, 2020.

2. Rebecca L. Thornton, "The Demand for, and Impact of, Learning HIV Status," *American Economic Review* 98, no. 5 (2008): 1829–1863; Esther Duflo, Pascaline Dupas, and Michael Kremer, "Education, HIV, and Early Fertility: Experimental Evidence from Kenya," *American Economic Review* 105, no. 9 (2015): 2757–2797.

3. Amalia R. Miller and Catherine Tucker, "Privacy Protection and Technology Diffusion: The Case of Electronic Medical Records," *Management Science* 55, no. 7 (2009): 1077–1093; Amalia R. Miller and Catherine Tucker, "Privacy Protection, Personalized Medicine, and Genetic Testing," *Management Science* 64, no. 10 (2018): 4648–4668.

4. Amalia R. Miller and Catherine Tucker, "Can Health Care Information Technology Save Babies?," *Journal of Political Economy* 119, no. 2 (2011): 289–324.

5. Susan Athey, Christian Catalini, and Catherine E. Tucker, "The Digital Privacy Paradox: Small Money, Small Costs, Small Talk," April 8, 2018, MIT Sloan Research Paper No. 5196-17; Stanford University Graduate School of Business Research Paper No. 17-14 (https://ssrn.com/abstract=2916489 or http://dx.doi.org/10.2139/ssrn.2916489).

6. While many countries have used isolation at home as a means of quarantine, East Asian countries have instead offered opting out of the

home quarantine to potentially great effect. See https://www.vox.com /2020/4/28/21238456/centralized-isolation-coronavirus-hong-kong-korea.

7. Of course, this relies on people being able to afford the resulting health-care. In the United States, where health insurance is not universal, this may be an additional constraint. Indeed, there is evidence that this matters when comparing the 1957–1958 and 1968–1969 pandemics; see Karen Clay, Joshua A. Lewis, Edson R. Severnini, and Xiao Wang, "The Value of Health Insurance during a Crisis: Effects of Medicaid Implementation on Pandemic Influenza Mortality," Working Paper No. 27120, NBER, May 2020.

8. See Martin S. Eichenbaum, Sergio Rebelo, and Mathias Trabandt, "The Macroeconomics of Testing and Quarantining," mimeo., Northwestern University, May 9, 2020; and Cameron Taylor, "Information and Risky Behavior: Model and Policy Implications for COVID-19," mimeo., Stanford University, June 6, 2020. See also Jonas Herby, "Paul Romer's Focus Is Wrong: The Problem Is Not Testing Capacity but Testing Participation," Working Paper No. 63, CEPOS, May 7, 2020.

9. Some have suggested that this could be achieved by giving people tickets in a weekly lottery. Steve Levitt, Paul Romer, and Jeff Severts, "How to Get Millions of People to Take Coronavirus Tests and Stay Home If They're Positive," USA Today, May 4, 2020 (https://www.usatoday.com/story/opin ion/2020/04/30/coronavirus-tests-quarantines-incentives-can-make-it -work-column/3048508001).

10. See Rahul Deb, Mallesh Pai, Akhil Vohra, and Rakesh Vohra, "Testing Alone Is Insufficient," mimeo., University of Toronto, May 6, 2020.

11. David Argente, Chang-Tai Hsieh, and Munseob Lee, "The Cost of Privacy: Welfare Effects of the Disclosure of Covid-19 Cases," May 14, 2020, University of Chicago, Becker Friedman Institute for Economics Working Paper No. 2020-64 (https://ssrn.com/abstract=3601143).

Chapter 9

1. The question mark is part of the name.

2. Neil Ferguson et al., *Report 9—Impact of Non-Pharmaceutical Interventions (NPIs) to Reduce COVID-19 Mortality and Healthcare Demand*, March 16, 2020 (https://www.imperial.ac.uk/mrc-global-infectious-disease-analysis /news--wuhan-coronavirus).

3. Pallab Ghosh, "Science Ponders 'Zombie Attack,'" *BBC News*, August 19, 2009 (http://news.bbc.co.uk/2/hi/science/nature/8206280.stm).

4. https://www.cdc.gov/cpr/zombie/index.htm.

5. If you want to know more about potential government response to zombies, I can recommend Daniel Drezner, *Theories of International Relations and Zombies* (Princeton University Press, 2011). He also presented an updated discussion in light of COVID-19: Daniel Drezner, "What I Learned about the Coronavirus World from Watching Zombie Flicks," *Foreign Affairs*, April 11, 2020 (https://foreignpolicy.com/2020/04/11/what-i-learned-about-coronavirus-world-from-zombie-movies). That piece ended with the hopeful thought, "Never count out a species responsible for duct tape."

6. Of course, it is also the case that merely removing a restriction may not lead to reopening. See Dylan Balla-Elliott, Zoë B. Cullen, Edward L. Glaeser, Michael Luca, and Christopher T. Stanton, "Business Reopening Decisions and Demand Forecasts During the COVID-19 Pandemic," Working Paper No. 27362, NBER, June 2020.

7. Jonathan Dingel and Brent Neiman, "How Many Jobs Can Be Done at Home?," mimeo., Becker Friedman Institute for Economics, University of Chicago, April 6, 2020 (https://bfi.uchicago.edu/working-paper/how-many-jobs-can-be-done-at-home); Erik Brynjolfsson, John Horton, Adam Ozimek, Daniel Rock, Garima Sharma, and Hong Yi Tu Ye, "COVID-19 and Remote Work: An Early Look at US Data," mimeo., MIT, April 8, 2020; and Simon Mongey, Laura Pilossoph, and Alex Weinberg, "Which Workers Bear the Burden of Social Distancing Policies?," mimeo., University of Chicago, April 26, 2020.

8. Some of these might be signaled by consumer behavior. One study showed that there was a positive correlation between locations where people had chosen to avoid prior to lockdowns and those locations that would be assessed as risky using other criteria; see Seth Benzell, Avinash Collis, and Christos Nicolaides, "Rationing Social Contact during the COVID-19 Pandemic: Transmission Risk and Social Benefits of US Locations," April 18, 2020 (https://ssrn.com/abstract=3579678).

9. For a good and accessible introduction to network theory, see Matthew O. Jackson, *The Human Network* (Pantheon, 2019).

10. A recent detailed study used a variety of data sources to show that the network structure differed enough between different cities in the United States to mean that distinct reopening policies should be followed. Mohammad Akbarpour, Cody Cook, Aude Marzuoli, Simon Mongey, Abhishek Nagaraj, Matteo Saccarolak, Pietro Tebaldi, and Shoshana Vasserman, "Socioeconomic Network Heterogeneity and Pandemic Policy Response," mimeo., University of California, Berkeley, June 9, 2020.

11. You can also identify hubs in the form of retail outlets that generate more physical interactions; see Avi Goldfarb and Catherine Tucker, "Which Retail Outlets Generate the Most Physical Interactions?," Working Paper No. 27042, NBER, April 2020.

12. Some jobs entail more high-intensity contact than others. See Fernando Leibovici, Ana Maria Santacreu, and Matthew Famigliettim, "Social Distancing and Contact-Intensive Occupations," *On the Economy Blog*, St. Louis Fed, March 24, 2020 (https://www.stlouisfed.org/on-the-economy /2020/march/social-distancing-contact-intensive-occupations).

13. Some economic modeling has shown that a "smart" reopening does not necessarily garner much improvement over a broad reopening and that the critical dimension is how strong social distancing and other protective behavior remains for nonwork social gatherings. See David Baqaee, Emmanuel Farhi, Michael J. Mina, and James H. Stock, "Reopening Scenarios," Working Paper No. 27244, NBER, May 2020.

14. Workplaces did not necessarily have to be told to take these measures. Walmart started to require temperature checks for employees with guaranteed pay if they were sent home (https://corporate.walmart.com /newsroom/2020/03/31/additional-steps-were-taking-for-the-health-and -safety-of-our-associates), while Amazon started to construct testing facilities at their workplaces (https://blog.aboutamazon.com/company-news /scalable-testing-for-coronavirus). These actions provide support that workplaces might (1) be able to pass a certification for safe practices or (2) choose protocols backed up by liability claims should they be found to be responsible for spreading the virus.

15. This was suggested in a report by Andrew Oswald and Nattavudh Powdthavee, "The Case for Releasing the Young from Lockdown," CAGE Policy Briefing, April 2020, University of Warwick. See also Adriano A. Rampini, "Sequential Lifting of COVID-19 Interventions with Population Heterogeneity," Working Paper No. 27063, NBER, April 2020.

16. Steven Roberts and Rabee Tourky, "Plan for Unlocking the Australian Economy during the COVID-19 Mobility Lockdowns," *Medium*, April 12, 2020 (https://medium.com/@rabeetourky/plan-for-unlocking-the-australian -economy-during-the-covid-19-mobility-lockdowns-9566af616564).

17. Debraj Ray and S. Subramanian, "Covid-19: Is There a Reasonable Alternative to a Comprehensive Lockdown?," *Ideas for India*, March 28, 2020 (https://www.ideasforindia.in/topics/macroeconomics/is-there-a-reason able-alternative-to-a-comprehensive-lockdown.html).

Chapter 10

1. Michael Kremer and Heidi Williams, "Incentivizing Innovation: Adding to the Tool Kit," *Innovation Policy and the Economy* 10, no. 1 (2010): 13.

2. Jacob Schmookler, *Invention and Economic Growth* (Harvard University Press, 1966).

3. Alberto Galasso and Hong Luo, "The One Good Thing Caused by COVID-19: Innovation," Working Knowledge, Harvard Business School, May 7, 2020 (https://hbswk.hbs.edu/item/the-one-good-thing-caused-by -covid-19-innovation).

4. Alberto Galasso and Hong Luo, "Risk-Mitigating Technologies: The Case of Radiation Diagnostic Devices," *Management Science* (forthcoming, 2020).

5. Kevin A. Bryan, Jorge Lemus, and Guillermo Marshall, "Innovation during a Crisis: Evidence from Covid-19," mimeo., University of Toronto, April 29, 2020.

6. It is not without its problems. For a recent discussion, see Joshua Gans and Andrew Leigh, *Innovation + Equality: Creating a Future That Is More Star Trek than Terminator* (MIT Press, 2019).

7. https://www.bloomberg.com/opinion/articles/2020-03-19/curing-a-pan demic-could-make-you-rich.

8. For more of this type of thing, see Jack Hirshleifer, "The Private and Social Value of Information and the Reward to Inventive Activity," in *Uncertainty in Economics* (Academic Press, 1978), 541–556.

9. See the recent survey by Pierre Azoulay and Danielle Li, "Scientific Grant Funding," Working Paper No. 26889, NBER, March 2020.

10. https://blogs.imf.org/2020/04/14/the-great-lockdown-worst-eco nomic-downturn-since-the-great-depression.

11. In September 2019, this was anticipated by the US White House Council of Economic Advisors, which produced a report on the need to accelerate vaccine development should a pandemic arise. This was months before one actually arose. https://www.whitehouse.gov/wp-content/uploads/2019 /09/Mitigating-the-Impact-of-Pandemic-Influenza-through-Vaccine-Inno vation.pdf.

12. Alex Tabarrok, "Why Human Challenge Trials Will Be Necessary to Get a Coronavirus Vaccine," *The National Interest*, May 10, 2020 (https:// nationalinterest.org/blog/coronavirus/why-human-challenge-trials-will -be-necessary-get-coronavirus-vaccine-152786).

13. Susan Athey, Michael Kremer, Christopher Snyder, and Alex Tabarrok, "In the Race for a Coronavirus Vaccine, We Must Go Big. Really, Really Big," *New York Times*, May 4, 2020 (https://www.nytimes.com/2020 /05/04/opinion/coronavirus-vaccine.html?action=click&module=Opinion &pgtype=Homepage).

14. Susan Athey, Kendall Hoyt, and Michael Kremer, "Everyone Wins from Vaccine Cooperation," *Project Syndicate*, May 14, 2020 (https://www .project-syndicate.org/commentary/covid19-vaccine-global-diversified -portfolio-by-susan-athey-et-al-2020-05).

15. https://en.wikipedia.org/wiki/Longitude_rewards.

16. Alex Tabarrok has been a forceful proponent for them to deal with COVID-19 innovation ("Grand Innovation Prizes to Address Pandemics: A Primer," COVID-19 Policy Brief, Mercatus Center, George Mason University, March 19, 2020, https://www.mercatus.org/publications/covid-19 -policy-brief-series/grand-innovation-prizes-address-pandemics-primer).

17. For more on these methods, see Nicholas Bloom, John Van Reenen, and Heidi Williams, "A Toolkit of Policies to Promote Innovation," *Journal of Economic Perspectives* 33, no. 3 (2019): 163–184.

18. For additional discussions of AMCs, see Michael Kremer, "Creating Markets for New Vaccines: Pt. 1, Rationale," and "Creating Markets for New Vaccines: Pt. 2, Design Issues," both in *Innovation Policy and the Economy*, vol. 1, ed. Adam Jaffe, Josh Lerner, and Scott Stern (MIT Press, 2001); Michael Kremer and Rachel Glennerster, *Strong Medicine: Creating Incentives for Pharmaceutical Research on Neglected Diseases* (Princeton University

Press, 2004); and Owen Barder, Michael Kremer, and Ruth Levine, *Making Markets for Vaccines: Ideas to Action* (Center for Global Development, 2005).

19. For a discussion of the potential vaccine alternatives and their diversity, see Derek Lowe, "Coronavirus Vaccine Prospects," *Science Translational Medicine*, April 15, 2020 (https://blogs.sciencemag.org/pipeline /archives/2020/04/15/coronavirus-vaccine-prospects).

20. Note that it is important for a technologically close innovation that the price actually be set rather than a per dose subsidy. Michael Kremer, Jonathan Levin, and Christopher Snyder ("Designing Advanced Market Commitments for New Vaccines" [2019], mimeo., Harvard University) show that this latter case may actually cause too little capacity to be built, as that will be sufficient for an innovator to appropriate what might be available to fund the product.

21. Michael Kremer, Jon Levin, and Chris Snyder, "Advance Market Commitments: Insights from Theory and Experience," *American Economic Association Papers and Proceedings*, 2020.

22. Athey, Kremer, Snyder, and Tabarrok, "In the Race for a Coronavirus Vaccine, We Must Go Big."

23. This is also the case for scientists themselves who tend to be reluctant to pronounce a treatment or approach as safe. Charles F. Manski and Aleksey Tetenov, "Statistical Decision Properties of Imprecise Trials Assessing COVID-19 Drugs," Working Paper No. 27293, NBER, June 2020.

24. For an account, see Tim Harford, *Adapt: Why Success Always Starts with Failure* (Picador, 2012).

25. Safi Bahcall, *Loonshots: How to Nurture the Crazy Ideas That Win Wars, Cure Diseases and Transform Industries* (St. Martin's Press, 2019).

26. This is perhaps most critically directed at the idea of vaccine platforms—that is, methods that can quickly generate vaccines for almost any virus. This is being pursued by organizations such as CEPI (https:// cepi.net/research_dev/technology).

27. Jennifer Kahn, "How Scientists Could Stop the Next Pandemic before It Starts," *Wired*, April 21, 2020 (https://www.nytimes.com/2020/04/21 /magazine/pandemic-vaccine.html).

28. Josh Lerner and Jean Tirole, "Efficient Patent Pools," *American Economic Review* 94, no. 3 (2004): 691–711; Josh Lerner and Jean Tirole,

"Public Policy toward Patent Pools," *Innovation Policy and the Economy* 8 (January 1, 2007): 157–186.

29. Phil Taylor, "AbbVie Won't Enforce Patents for COVID-19 Drug Candidate Kaletra," *PharmaPhorum*, March 25, 2020 (https://pharmaphorum .com/news/abbvie-wont-enforce-patents-for-covid-19-drug-candidate -kaletra).

30. Something similar has been proposed for COVID-19; see Pierre Azoulay and Benjamin Jones, "Beat COVID-19 through Innovation," *Science* 368, no. 6491 (May 8, 2020): 553.

31. Iain M. Cockburn, Scott Stern, and Jack Zausner, "Finding the Endless Frontier: Lessons from the Life Sciences Innovation System for Energy R&D," in *Accelerating Energy Innovation: Insights from Multiple Sectors* (University of Chicago Press, 2011), 113–157.

32. Ajay Agrawal, Joshua Gans, Avi Goldfarb, and Mara Lederman, "The CEO's Guide to Safely Reopening the Workplace," *MIT Technology Review*, May 28, 2020.

Chapter 11

1. Elena Conis, Michael McCoyd, and Jessir Moravek, "What to Expect When a Coronavirus Vaccine Finally Arrives," *New York Times*, May 20, 2020 (https://www.nytimes.com/2020/05/20/opinion/coronavirus-vaccine -polio.html).

2. Martin L. Weitzman, "Is the Price System or Rationing More Effective in Getting a Commodity to Those Who Need It Most?," *The Bell Journal of Economics* (1977): 517–524.

3. https://www.cdc.gov/flu/pandemic-resources/pdf/2018-Influenza-Gui dance.pdf.

4. This example comes from work thinking about how to use different criteria to ration other items in short supply like ventilators. The idea is to allow people to self-select what criteria might be appropriate and then use methods developed in market design—specifically, matching markets—to determine the ration order. See Parag Pathak, Tayfun Sonmez, M. Utku Unver, and M. Bumin Yenmez, "Triage Protocol Design for Ventilator Rationing in a Pandemic: A Proposal to Integrate Multiple Ethical Values through Reserves," mimeo., MIT, April 2020 (http://economics.mit.edu

/files/19358). Another option is to broaden the ability to share ventilators across regions; see Simon Loertscher and Leslie M. Marx, "A National Ventilator Exchange Could Address Critical Shortages," *The Hill*, March 27, 2020 (https://thehill.com/opinion/healthcare/489858-a-national-ventilator -exchange-could-address-critical-shortages).

5. One advantage from a random allocation via lottery is that it makes it easier to evaluate any potential side-effects from a vaccine something that is not possible if doses are allocated according to a defined list.

6. Yeon-Koo Che, Ian Gale, and Jinwoo Kim, "Assigning Resources to Budget-Constrained Agents," *Review of Economic Studies* 80, no. 1 (2013): 73–107. In addition, this paper shows that giving a subsidy to low-wealth individuals prior to having a market process for obtaining vaccines can achieve some of the same benefits as a lottery with resale.

7. A similar effect occurs when sports leagues give priority in drafts of new players to teams who have performed poorly.

8. Scott Kominers, Parag Pathak, Tayfun Sonmez, and M. Utku Unver, "Paying It Backward and Forward: Expanding Access to Convalescent Plasma Therapy Using Market Design," mimeo., Harvard University, May 2020 (http://economics.mit.edu/files/19708).

9. I should note that both of these options would likely work better if these vouchers could be resold.

Chapter 12

1. John Maynard Keynes, *The Economic Consequences of the Peace* (Macmillan, 1921).

2. https://www.ted.com/talks/bill_gates_the_next_outbreak_we_re_not _ready?language=en#t-442139.

3. Ian W. R. Martin and Robert S. Pindyck, "Averting Catastrophes: The Strange Economics of Scylla and Charybdis," *American Economic Review* 105, no. 10 (2015): 2947–2985.

4. Martin and Pindyck, "Averting Catastrophes," 2948.

5. For catastrophes, it is surely no better to add up the value of lives than thinking about the value of those lives together, which is likely to be a much different calculation. Nonetheless, in a recent paper, Ian Martin and

Bob Pindyck do take that approach in better accounting for death in their calculations; see Ian Martin and Robert Pindyck, "Welfare Costs of Catastrophes: Lost Consumption and Lost Lives," *Economic Journal*, forthcoming.

6. https://www.statista.com/statistics/534123/e-commerce-share-of-retail-sales-worldwide.

7. Autor quoted in Sarah Leeson, "The Economics of a Global Emergency," WGBH News, April 17, 2020 (https://www.wgbh.org/news/national-news/2020/04/17/the-economics-of-a-global-emergency).

8. See Barthélémy Bonadio, Zhen Huo, Andrei A. Levchenko, and Nitya Pandalai-Nayar, "Global Supply Chains in the Pandemic," Working Paper No. 27224, NBER, May 2020.

9. Another flaw for both the British and the French was, despite having invented the tank in World War I, they still invested in warfare based on the horse. Tim Harford, "Why Big Companies Squander Good Ideas," *Financial Times*, September 6, 2018 (https://www.ft.com/content/3c1ab748-b09b-11e8-8d14-6f049d06439c).

10. See my book on the subject, *The Disruption Dilemma* (MIT Press, 2016).

11. For a discussion of this, see Robert Meyer and Howard Kunreuther, *The Ostrich Paradox: Why We Underprepare for Disasters* (Wharton School Press, 2017).

12. This does not mean that there won't be some adjustment of beliefs regarding pandemics (see Julian Kozlowski, Laura Veldkamp, and Venky Venkateswaran, "Scarring Body and Mind: The Long-Term Belief-Scarring Effects of COVID-19," Working Paper, No.27439, NBER, June 2020). The question is whether that adjustment will be enough to lead to action.

About the Author

Joshua Gans is a Professor of Strategic Management and holder of the Jeffrey S. Skoll Chair of Technical Innovation and Entrepreneurship at the Rotman School of Management, University of Toronto (with a cross appointment in the Department of Economics). Since 2013, he has been Chief Economist of the Creative Destruction Lab. Prior to 2011, he was the foundation Professor of Management (Information Economics) at the Melbourne Business School, University of Melbourne, and prior to that he was at the School of Economics, University of New South Wales. In 2011, Joshua was a visiting researcher at Microsoft Research (New England). Joshua holds a PhD from Stanford University and an honors degree in economics from the University of Queensland. In 2012, Joshua was appointed as a Research Associate of the NBER in the Productivity, Innovation and Entrepreneurship Program.

At Rotman, he teaches MBA and Commerce students Entrepreneurial Strategy. He has also coauthored (with Stephen King and Robin Stonecash) the Australasian edition of Greg Mankiw's *Principles of Economics* (published by Cengage), *Core Economics for Managers* (Cengage), *Finishing the Job* (Melbourne University Publishing), *Parentonomics* (MIT Press), *Information Wants to Be Shared* (Harvard

Business Review Press), *The Disruption Dilemma* (MIT Press), *Prediction Machines: The Simple Economics of Artificial Intelligence* (Harvard Business Review Press), and *Innovation + Equality* (MIT Press).

While Joshua's research interests are varied, he has developed specialties in the nature of technological competition and innovation, economic growth, publishing economics, industrial organization, and regulatory economics. This has culminated in publications in the *American Economic Review, Journal of Political Economy, RAND Journal of Economics, Journal of Economic Perspectives, Journal of Public Economics*, and the *Journal of Regulatory Economics*. Joshua serves as department editor of *Management Science* and the *Journal of Industrial Economics* and is on the editorial boards of the *Economic Analysis and Policy* and *Games*. In 2007, Joshua was awarded the Economic Society of Australia's Young Economist Award. In 2008, Joshua was elected as a Fellow of the Academy of Social Sciences, Australia. He has also written for the *Financial Times, Sloan Management Review*, and other outlets with over 200 opinion pieces.